Richard Wilmer

The recent past from a southern standpoint

Reminiscences of a grandfather. Second Edition

Richard Wilmer

The recent past from a southern standpoint
Reminiscences of a grandfather. Second Edition

ISBN/EAN: 9783337222635

Printed in Europe, USA, Canada, Australia, Japan

Cover: Foto ©ninafisch / pixelio.de

More available books at **www.hansebooks.com**

Yours faithfully,
Rich'd H. Wilmer
Bishop of Alabama

THE RECENT PAST

FROM A SOUTHERN STANDPOINT.

Reminiscences of a Grandfather.

"FORSAN ET HÆC OLIM MEMINISSE JUVABIT."

BY

RICHARD H. WILMER,

BISHOP OF ALABAMA.

SECOND EDITION.

NEW YORK:
THOMAS WHITTAKER,
2 AND 3 BIBLE HOUSE.
1887.

RAND AVERY COMPANY,
ELECTROTYPERS AND PRINTERS,
BOSTON.

THIS VOLUME IS DEDICATED TO

The Cause of Truth, Right, and Peace,

IN LOVING MEMORY OF
ALL WHO GAVE THEIR LIVES FOR ITS MAINTENANCE;
AND IN BROTHERLY RECOGNITION OF ALL
WHO LIVE TO VINDICATE AND
DEFEND IT.

"The wisdom which cometh from above is first pure, then peaceable."

TITLE.

WHEN I had concluded to give public expression to the thoughts contained herein, I found it difficult to determine upon a title for the volume. Publishers told me that the country was flooded with "Reminiscences," and that the people took no interest in them, and that "there is every thing in the name."

I first thought I would call it "Old Mortality;" forgetting, for the moment, that that name had been illuminated and immortalized by the genius of Scott. So I had to abandon that idea. Yet it will be found that in these "Reminiscences," I have plied the same vocation with "Old Mortality." As was his wont, I have been going lovingly and reverently among the graves of our heroic and sainted dead. It has been a grateful task for me to pluck a nettle here, and plant a flower instead; with sharp incision to freshen up some fading inscription; to remove the moss and lichen with which time was incrusting them, and cause the very gravestones once more — In Memoriam — to speak aloud the names and deeds of those who, in our hearts and memories, should never die.

Let this my purpose incline the youth of this generation to dwell fondly upon "Reminiscences" dedicated to "the Cause and Maintenance of Truth, Right, and Peace."

CONTENTS.

	PAGE
PRELIMINARY	9
LOYALTY	16
CITIZENSHIP	20
THE CONSTITUTION	24
WAR OF THE STATES	27
DOMESTIC SLAVERY	37
"UNCLE TOM'S CABIN"	41
THE CHURCH QUESTION	49
CHURCH IN ENGLAND	52
CHURCH IN AMERICA	57
HOW THE CHURCH WAS PLANTED IN AMERICA	59
JOHN STEWART OF VIRGINIA	67
DIFFERENT RELIGIOUS BODIES IN THE UNITED STATES	83
ROMAN, OR LATIN, CHURCH	87
THE PRESBYTERIAN COMMUNION	93
BAPTIST FRIENDS	99
THE METHODISTS	111
CONCLUSION OF MATTERS PERTAINING TO RELIGIOUS ORGANIZATIONS	114
SCEPTICISM, RATIONALISM, AND SCIENTISM	118
POST-BELLUM REMINISCENCES	139
INTRUSION OF THE MILITARY POWER	139
RE-UNION OF THE CHURCHES NORTH AND SOUTH	147

CONTENTS.

	PAGE
A REPLY TO BISHOP HOPKINS'S CIRCULAR LETTER TO THE SOUTHERN BISHOPS, BY ONE OF THEIR NUMBER	153
NOTE BY BISHOP GREEN	166
REV. WILLIAM H. WILMER, D.D.	166
REMINISCENCES OF RIGHT REV. J. P. B. WILMER, D.D., LL.D., LATE BISHOP OF LOUISIANA	180
THE LATE BISHOP ELLIOTT OF GEORGIA	201
REMINISCENCES OF THE RIGHT REV. NICHOLAS HAMNER COBBS, D.D.	242
CONCLUSION	271
APPENDIX	278

REMINISCENCES OF A GRANDFATHER

PRELIMINARY.

"Now the days of King David drew nigh that he should die; and he charged Solomon his son, saying, I go the way of all the earth: be thou strong therefore, and shew thyself a man; and keep the charge of the Lord thy God, to walk in His ways, to keep His statutes, and His commandments, and His judgments, and His testimonies, as it is written in the law of Moses, that thou mayest prosper in all that thou doest, and whithersoever thou turnest thyself."

MAN, as the things of time recede from sight, and he is preparing to depart for his long home, would fain stamp immortality upon something. The thought of annihilation is fearful. If his own life has been a failure, he will hope that his posterity may make amends for his own misdoings: if his life has yielded any good fruit, he may hope that they will bring it to perfection.

With some such feelings I have jotted down, from time to time, the incidents and reflections contained in these "Reminiscences." At the time of writing them, I had no view to publication, as will appear from their personal character and familiar style. I thought, that, after I had gone the way of all the earth, my children and children's children would derive pleasure and profit from knowing the thoughts of one whose memory they cherished, and who had lived a long life during an eventful period of the country's history.

But some friends, — partial friends, perhaps, — who have run their eyes over the manuscript, warmly urge its publication, saying that no existing book covers exactly the same ground with these "Reminiscences." Yielding to their wishes, I send the volume forth, to add a drop more to the flood of publications which is sweeping on to swift and sure oblivion.

There is one word which I must say at the outset, in order that my language and position may be clearly understood and fairly interpreted.

I speak plainly of matters political, sectional, social, and ecclesiastical — of Northern and Southern men, etc. The spurious charity of these latter days demands from me a degree of reticence, caution, and suppression which I have not exercised in these pages, and which I deem utterly inconsistent with that divine charity which "rejoiceth in the truth." Men are not candid enough with each other. They will attack each other in secret, but they will not talk face to face. This may beget a sort of love, and pass for charity, but it is not the love which is "without dissimulation." In my judgment, many errors abound, and acquire a sort of respectability because they are not candidly and charitably exposed. Truth is not so hard to find as men think. Error is founded in ignorance, prejudice, pride, and passion. Let "knowledge with fervent charity" prevail, and men will be drawn nearer together in heart and mind. All else will fail save charity. Temporary fraternizations, — such as those among the denominations, — where all consent to suppress some conviction by way of a truce, discard the very element of love which "rejoiceth in the truth." Aggregations of men bound together by mechanical appliances only, fall to pieces for the want of that cement of love which is "the very bond of peace and of all virtues."

Judged by the modern ideas of charity, I trust that I shall be condemned as an uncharitable man, for I enjoy the ill judgment of some people; but, judged by a higher standard, I hope to stand acquitted before God, even as I am in all conscience, for "rejoicing in the truth."

When, then, in these pages I speak of the North and Northern men, I have not in my eye that large body of people whose culture, refinement, and large-hearted generosity challenge my admiration, and has oftentimes elicited my personal gratitude. "*O, si sic omnes!*" But I speak of that fanatical, and at times dominant, element, which having waged a destructive war (and for that it becomes me to make no moan), and after having destroyed our wealth, and laid waste our territory, and revolutionized our domestic and political life, persistently aims at our humiliation, still plies us with ignominious epithets, and, to use a vulgar current phrase, "still waves the bloody shirt."

I was written to some years ago by an editor of the North, who wished to know the reason for the solidarity of the South, and whether I, in my position, could not write or do something to dissolve it. He must have been "an innocent," or thought me one. The weather at the time was cold beyond precedent, and our waters were frozen over. I replied to him in one sentence: "The solidarity of the South is due to the same cause that just now makes our water solid, — unfriendly breezes from the North."

Again, when I speak of "denominational bodies of Christians," I have not in view that noble army of learned, devout, and zealous Christians of nearly all names, whom I feel all too unworthy to call brethren; for I would love to sit at the feet of some of those men, and learn from them how to be more like our common Lord and Saviour, by Whose blood we were all redeemed, and of Whose life, I trust, I am partaker with them. No! I have not such men in my eye; they are of the "Brotherhood," whom I am glad to love; and my very love for them causes me to contend for, and rejoice in, the truth, which would bring us all together, and make us one in Christ Jesus, even as He and the Father are One. Then we should not, as unhappily we are now doing, "*live apart*," but "*dwell together*" in unity.

No! I am speaking of communities — humanly organized, as they appear to my eye — which, without adequate cause or warranty, have created sects and divisions in Christendom, thereby breaking the line of the Church Militant, and enfeebling its power of resisting the combined power of Satan and his hosts. His kingdom is not divided. The divided Church feels now the force of the shock from his concentrated assaults. I speak earnestly and in unmistakable language on this point. We cannot promote unity by thinking or speaking lightly of divisions among Christians. No malignant evil was ever remedied by treating it as a matter of no consequence. If there be ever any real movement towards Christian unity, it must be preceded by some clear and distinct conviction of the nature, causes, and guilt of schism.

Meanwhile "this Church" of ours, recognizing every baptized man as a member of Christ, offers to meet Christendom on the broad platform of the Holy Scriptures, the ancient Creeds, the divinely ordered Sacraments, and the Apostolical ministry. Rome would meet us there to-day by discarding her new doctrines, and becoming catholic, as she once was. But I am somewhat anticipating.

One chief reason for giving these reminiscences to the public, is that I may help to keep sacred in the memory of the rising generation the traditions of their fathers. A new generation ordinarily little cares for, and little acquaints itself with, the past. This results in part from the fact that ordinarily parents concern themselves too little with the opinions of their children on matters past, present, or to come. I do not share this indifference. I have a special fear that our young people, as they recede farther and farther from our times, will gather their views of the recent past from partisan histories rather than from sacredly preserved traditions. The school-books and histories of our times are, as a general rule, from Northern sources: their authors naturally look at all these matters with other eyes than ours. I cannot endure to think that any descendant of mine shall open, say, a catechism, and find Benedict Arnold, Jefferson Davis, and Robert E. Lee chosen out to exemplify Treason and Rebellion. It was bruited abroad that there was such a catechism, but I can hardly believe without ocular demonstration. I want our young people to know what I know, — that the two men last named in the list of "traitors" were men who exemplified through life every trait of honor and loyalty.

Nor can I endure to think that my grandsons shall be set down to read histories which tell them that their ancestors were "tyrants to their servants," "rebels against their government," and "traitors to their country." So far as in me lies, this shall never be; and shame to every man who loves not to pluck the nettles from the graves of his sires, and strew them with flowers!

As it regards myself, I have saved much time and correspondence by putting these thoughts in print. To every-day letters and inquiries, I shall be enabled to say, "Here in this volume is what I think upon such matters." We have in our midst many earnest and ingenuous young men, who respect the memory of their fathers, some of whom, alas! are buried on unknown battle-fields. They come to me, and say, "My father is, stigmatized in these books and newspapers as a 'rebel' and a 'traitor:' how is this?" — "Well, my son," say I, "if your father was a rebel, I was one, and so was every cultured man of the Far

South, almost without exception. Here in these 'Reminiscences' is our view of this matter."

I suppose that few will read these pages, save those who sympathize with my views. To such persons I am enabled to say, if you wish your children to understand and reverence the traditions of our people, you may possibly find in this volume some thoughts that may help to keep green in their memories the days of "Auld Lang Syne," and warm and sacred in their hearts recollections of "*The Old Folks at Home.*"

LOYALTY.

THE thoughts, which I now submit for consideration in the following pages, were written for your eyes alone, and not with any idea of publication. Whilst writing my will, and leaving some few injunctions to you, the question came across my mind, Why should not a father tell his children more of his opinions of the times in which he lived, and thus enable them to gather his views upon questions of deep concernment to all generations? Following out this thought, I have herein set down for your consideration the conclusions which I, in common with men of my class and position, have reached upon matters — some of them, at least — of enduring interest. You are now reading, and will continue to read, the histories of the past and present day; but you cannot gather with satisfaction the tone and temper of an age from any general history. We glean from some works of fiction — say Scott's novels — clearer ideas of the times of which they are written, than you can possibly do from any general history of the same era. It is quite notable that Scott's novels are hardly fictions, and his history of Napoleon is almost a falsehood. Scott's genius has illuminated his native land through his novels.

It is commonly said that one generation can only bequeath knowledge and treasure to that succeeding it. This is, in the main, true. Wisdom is to be won in the battle of life, each gaining it for himself. Knowledge is cumulative; so is wealth. But when children ponder lovingly the thoughts of their forefathers, there must be some small residuum of *wisdom* deposited besides the *knowledge* gained. At all events, I have given you these reminiscences in the hope that I may — not fetter the minds of my descendants, for they should be wiser than he who writes these lines, but — keep them on the right track of thought, and hold them true and loyal to the traditions of their forefathers. This sentiment of loyalty is a necessary part of an integral character, as is conscience, although, like conscience, liable to be ill instructed, misguided, and even perverted. One cannot be a whole man, who is without loyalty. It is the cement of home, the bond of society, the defence of states, — yea! the essence of piety. To cherish it, and guide it, and instruct it, is a large part of education.

Loyalty does not hold one slavishly and unquestioningly to the traditions of one's family and country, for then men could never change and never improve. And there is, necessarily, no violation of loyalty in departing from transmitted and hereditary ideas. For if one changes the opinions which he received by inheritance, because convinced that his ideas were not well founded in truth, and takes hold of those things which he believes to be true, howsoever at variance with inherited convictions, such a one is, in the highest sense, *loyal* — loyal to Him who is Truth. The lower gives way to the higher; the less gives place to the greater; the reverence for the earthly merges in the reverence due the heavenly — as the moon and stars become invisible when the sun rules the day. Therefore I like it not when I hear it said, "I will not go back upon my father's or my mother's opinions or creed." The sentiment which inspires such declarations is most praiseworthy; but if the parents unfortunately were in error (and the best parents, as all admit, are liable to err), it binds one to error, which is disloyalty to truth. Thus, a misguided loyalty may end in actual treason. Better to say, "My parents, with the light they had, held such and such an opinion. With the light before me, I cannot hold the same opinion. With my light, they would, in all probability, have come to a different opinion. I cannot go back upon them, but I must go forward from them, and move with the ever-moving world nearer the 'Father of Lights,' with Whom, and Whom alone, there is no 'variableness or shadow of turning.'" I write this much that my children may not misunderstand me in what I shall hereinafter advise them. I shall give them my counsel, and I know that they will weigh it well; and this is all that I can properly claim at their hands. I only wish them to be clear in this; viz., "Follow truth and right always." That means to follow Him Who is the Truth. That is the meaning of that mighty declaration, "Whosoever shall love any thing — houses, lands, father and mother, wife and children — more than Me, is not worthy of Me." The world might exist without the light of the planets, but how without the light of the life-giving sun? He who most loves the truth and the right, will most honor his parents, for honor and reverence to parents is a part of the truth. The whole of the truth is very vast indeed. Draw near to it, my children, embrace it, cleave steadfastly unto it; let its arms be around thy neck, its kiss upon thy forehead; plant thy feet upon it, and let it be a crown of glory to thy head. As thou art *true*, so shalt *thou* be.

CITIZENSHIP.

LET us look around about us. Perhaps I should begin more properly with the individual, and talk to you about the *man*, his body, soul, and spirit. If I live to complete this letter, I may, perhaps, touch all these several points. But just now I feel more disposed to treat and get rid of certain matters of a more general description, hoping that as I get nearer the end of life, and get more of the light that streams from the "Delectable Mountains," I may have more to tell you of that other country for which we are all bound, and on the confines of which I know that I am now standing. Of this, more anon. I want now to say something about your *earthly citizenship*. No man liveth to himself. He is a member of society, and under government. The books of history and geography which you may read will give you all that you need to know in a general way about the several continents and countries, etc. I let all that pass, only observing that histories, as a general rule, are one-sided, partisan, and partial, recording the facts from many various and conflicting stand-points, insomuch that we are often compelled, with Pilate, to exclaim, "What is truth?" To go into this matter (at any sufficient length to make it profitable), I find impracticable. Let it suffice for me to say this much: The history of one age is pretty much the history of all ages; that which hath been, is now, and until something, as yet unknown to history, shall intervene, will most likely continue to be; and there is, so far as human nature is concerned, "nothing new under the sun."

There is one matter about which I feel especially solicitous that you should be rightly informed; and that is, the political history of your own country, and section of country. We have passed through, during the last twenty-five years, a mighty revolution. That revolution effected a mighty change in the character of our government and institutions. It is most important for you to understand the merits of that conflict of ideas which convulsed the minds of the people, North and South, and finally culminated in a sectional war, which turned a million of men to ashes, and covered the whole land with mourning. Even at this present moment, as I write, we seem to walk on molten lava, whose surface is scarcely cooled. Your father, who is writing these lines, was deeply and passionately involved on the side of his State and section; ready, if his ministerial calling had not forbidden, to have shouldered his musket, and entered the fight. As it was, under a temporary access of passion, he became captain of a home-guard, and drilled daily, while yet rector of a church near Richmond, Va. I mention this to give you an idea of the intensity of the excitement. Your grand-uncle, the Rev. Lemuel Wilmer, who was, as he viewed it, an ardent patriot, wrote me after the war was over, that, when Maryland was invaded, he went to Washington with musket on his shoulder, and took his place in the trenches. He was then an old man, and had been rector of Port Tobacco Parish for half a century. I refer to this incident to show you that some of our blood still live up to the motto on the family coat-of-arms, — "*Facit quod suscipit.*" A little reflection served to cool the heat of my fever, and turned my attention to a more legitimate sphere of action. Besides, I read that the "Son of man" — whose servant I was — "came, not to *destroy* men's lives, but to *save* them;" and I read also, that "the *servant must be as his lord.*" While the war lasted, I did what I could for the wounded and the sick, and blew the trumpet to excite men to action in the field; taking as my warranty for doing this much, the permission given to the Jewish Priesthood, "to blow the silver trumpets in case of a war of invasion." You will have read, and will continue to read, as they are published, many histories of that conflict. I do not wish to so bias your minds as that they shall not take a calmer, and perhaps clearer, view of that conflict of ideas and of arms than I, from my position, could be expected to do. Your own views on this matter will, and must, depend, in great measure, upon the description of books that you are likely to read. Owing to the fact that the North does most of the publishing of books,—and especially of school-books,—you will most likely at school be in a situation to imbibe Northern ideas of the origin, causes, etc., of the whole revolution; to hear many whose names have stood high for learning, character, and for all that makes up true nobility, characterized as "rebels," "traitors," and the like; and a great, though ineffectual, struggle for right and compact denounced as "The *Great Rebellion.*" Well, if all this was as our enemies allege, I have no wish to so forestall your minds with opinions to the contrary as to close them to the entrance of the truth. For truth, like the King's messenger, has authority to enter the mind and the heart "*in the name of the King.*" Our only privilege is, to inquire whether it is the King's messenger. To guide you in such an inquiry, and to dictate not at all, is the object of this writing.

THE CONSTITUTION.

When we look back to the early history of the United States, we find that certain colonies, peopled from the British Isles for the most part, were stretched along the Atlantic coast. Disaffection sprang up among the colonists, principally because of taxes laid upon the people, without privilege of representation. By little and little, they came at last to war. The conflict was waged with varying fortunes for some years. Epithets of "rebels" and "traitors," etc., were as freely applied to our forefathers on the part of the Mother Country, as by the North to ourselves in our so-called "Rebellion." The issue, as you know, was decided in favor of the revolting colonies, whose "Declaration of Independence" was made good by the arbitrament of war. These colonies, thus set free to govern themselves (their independence as separate States having been acknowledged by Great Britain), soon began to cast about for an alliance among themselves closer than that of the "Articles of Confederation" which they had adopted. The materials to be united were in some respects heterogeneous, their interests somewhat conflicting, and their ideas of the government to be formed widely variant. However, after much debate, they finally united under the "Constitution of the United States," — the same instrument that now exists, except (besides some amendments made soon after its adoption) the important and radical changes which resulted from the war between the States. I do' not purpose going into a minute history of the events which led to this consummation, nor to touch upon the original differences of opinion which required to be harmonized and adjusted before the Constitution found general acceptance and adoption. Two quite equally divided parties struggled for the mastery, — the one contended for a strong central government, the other for a more decided recognition of the sovereignty of the several States. The result was a Constitution which aimed to embody both features, and it required a bloody war to settle the meaning of the Constitution. In other words, the party which could bring the greatest number of soldiers into the field had their own way in interpreting the meaning of the Constitution, and thus, practically, the question concerning the *power* to secede was for the time determined; the question of original *right* under the Constitution not being, by gunpowder, determinable.

Let me digress for a moment at this point, to pay my willing tribute to the genius of Alexander Hamilton, in my judgment, the largest-minded statesman that this continent has produced. Hamilton was the leader of the Federal party, and contended for a government with such centripetal power that it could not fly to pieces in the revolution of affairs. Had his principles fully obtained, and been ingrafted in the Constitution, — or, rather, had been made the framework of the same, — questions of secession could not have well arisen, or at least could not have arisen upon an interpretation of the Constitution. His broad views of human affairs, and his far-seeing sagacity, taught him that all confederated sovereignties tended to consolidation. His views, if they had to the full prevailed, would have rendered impossible the agitation of secession, as a right under the Constitution. Consolidation has taken place, but by war. He wanted it to take place, and to hold its place, by original formation. His ounce of prevention would have saved many pounds of cure. The history of nations, without exception, goes to show that there is no longevity in confederated or united sovereignties, — in proof, the Saxon Heptarchy, the principalities of Germany, the republics of Italy, the Dukedoms of France, etc. But Hamilton's views did not wholly prevail. All such differences as existed between him and the opposite party were settled by the adoption of a compromise Constitution, recognizing enough of State sovereignty to keep up the idea of separate and independent action on the part of the several States, and, at the same time, absorbing so much power, defined or implied in the Federal Government, as to cripple the States, and render them helpless in an hour when they might attempt to redress a wrong, or, if that seemed hopeless, to fly for safety — secede was the word used to express the idea. Whether the original Constitution was the best that could have been framed, is one question; how it was really made, is quite another. Had the idea of the Federalists prevailed fully, the question of right to secede could never have arisen. But it did not fully prevail. Thus, antagonistic views existed as germs in the very Constitution itself, and bayonets were called in to skewer the people together. An examination of the present Constitution as amended by war has somewhat of a *post-mortem* character.

WAR OF THE STATES.

But how came the Southern States to secede, and which section of the country must bear the responsibility of the work of its consequent horrors? A vast question indeed, and one upon which libraries will be written before new events shall have buried this question among other dead issues.

The ablest and fairest exposition of this question, in my judgment, is from the pen of Jefferson Davis, President of the Confederate States while they lasted. It is a calm and statesmanlike review of the whole subject-matter. Davis will be pilloried in Northern histories as an "arch-rebel," and traitorous to the core. So much for the truth of partisan history! While, on the contrary, his whole history will show that he was a calm, clear-headed, and large-hearted man, chosen in the hour of need for his known merits, and on the strength of his history, which was not obscure nor ignoble. That he failed, was not extraordinary; that he held out so long, was the marvel. I write from much knowledge of the man. If you would understand him and the history of his times, read his book, "The Rise and Fall of the Southern Confederacy,"—unanswered and unanswerable, as we of the South think.

But there was a feature in the history of the Southern struggle for independence which you must understand in order to do justice to your ancestors in regard to the part which they felt constrained by their interest, by their sense of personal self-respect, and by their loyalty, to maintain to the end.

Slavery existed in the United States at an early day. It was not confined to the Southern section. Northern vessels brought the slaves from Africa, and they were held in bondage whenever it was found profitable to hold them. The climate of the South best suited the native African, and his labor was found more profitable upon a Southern soil. Consequently, the larger population of slaves were gathered in the Southern section of this country. They constituted the greater part of the wealth of the Southern States. Their status must be provided for in the Constitution, and thus a guaranty be afforded that the Southern States should be protected in the possession of their property. For a while things went on smoothly; but, very soon, strong and fanatical ideas began to take possession of Northern minds. It manifested itself in every possible way, — in efforts to legislate slavery out of the District of Columbia; in efforts to circumscribe the area of slavery by excluding it from the Territories, the common home and property of the peoples of all the States; in incendiary pamphlets; in books of fiction; in books for the school-room; in organizations for kidnapping slaves, and helping them to their freedom; in fierce debates upon the floors of Congress, and at last in an invasion by armed men of the soil of Virginia, with implements of war to arm the emancipated slave. This last event occurred in October, 1859. And there are living men who enroll the leader of that murderous band in the noble Army of Martyrs. *God help them!* Up to this time the General Government had committed itself to no act which could be construed as offensive and aggressive towards the South. But events rapidly progressed. The abolition spirit had grown with great rapidity and intensity. It soon became a political power, then a political party, and finally succeeded in electing a President upon a platform of principles which was undisguisedly hostile to Southern institutions and property. With the more violent members of the "*Republican*" party, — for such was their name, — the "*Constitution*" of the country (a solemn compact between the States, and the sole guaranty under which the Southern States held their institutions) was denounced as a "*Covenant with Hell*," because it protected the South in their property. In some instances State legislation obstructed by penal laws the restoration of slaves, a right to which had been secured in the Constitution. The question now arose, — and it was a question so large, and involving so much that was dear and valuable, that it stirred every heart, — "What shall we do? Hitherto we have been able to appeal to the General Government. That Government will soon be in the hands of men, the most violent of whom will without scruple invade our rights." "Shall we secede, and live to ourselves?" said the believers in the right of secession. "Shall we wait, and see whether the incendiary will apply his torch?" said the more timid and cautious. "Shall we go out from the Union as separate States, or shall we act with others?" said the more wary co-operant. "Shall we wait until we receive the blow, or shall we give it ourselves?" said the multitude. Such were the questions that agitated every family circle throughout the country. People answered this question, as people always do, according to their kind — each after his own order. Some thoughtful and far-seeing men saw at a glance that if a movement were to be made, it should be made at once. They argued, that, if you saw a man about to enter your premises with harsh and dangerous intent, it would not be wise to wait until he had struck you down before you took measures of self-defence; and they contended that the attitude of the Republican party, now for the first time in power, with all their past history and utterances to interpret their intended deeds, was hostile, and would be aggressive, and that the Constitution of the country would no longer be a shield and defence to them. But, on the other hand, there were other men, equally sincere, who loved the Union with a deep devotion (such men as Bishop Meade and General Lee), and who were willing to sacrifice all, save honor, to their country's cause. In a word, some were for going out at once, some for waiting, some for temporizing, some few for yielding. Meanwhile, events moved fast. State after State seceded. The believers in State sovereignty esteemed it loyalty to follow the action of their respective States. Following the logical sequence, they scrupled not to seize upon the fortresses at the mouths of their harbors. They argued, and with reason, that these fortresses were erected for the defence of the cities which they protected; they were builded in part with the money of the people whose interests they were designed to guard, and were the common property of the States which they respectively defended. Now, it looked as if the General Government was about to use these forts to injure the Southern States. They were proceeding to garrison and provision them for war,—notably, the Fortress of Sumter, which protected the city of Charleston, and also commanded the city with its guns. The Federal Government manœuvred so as to make the South seem to take the initiative in the conflict. By an attempt to re-enforce Fort Sumter, which, in effect, meant to batter down Charleston, they compelled the Southern troops to fire the first gun, and thus secured the prestige which, on the surface, made the South appear to be the aggressive party. This fired the whole North, brought out a proclamation for troops by the President of the United States, and thus was fired in turn the heart of the South; and the whole country was plunged into a sectional war with an intensity of passion which has seldom, if ever, had its parallel in history. All thought of continued Union vanished from the mildest and most conservative men. Henceforth the Union man in the South was reckoned to be traitorous, and was so branded. In the Far South, with the exception of a very few, every Southern man of honor and character and standing ranged himself under the banner of his own State. The whole country was in arms, and very soon, as the histories of the time will show, in mourning. The war was fierce, bloody, and protracted. The issue, although at times looking favorable to the South, was not long doubtful. The North had population, arms, and access to the world. The Southern ports were blockaded, powder had to be made or smuggled, and she was shut out from the world to her own resources. Besides, her population, originally smaller than that of the

North, was divided. Nearly all of the Southern
border States furnished men to the Federal Government; and, in the progress of the war, the
negroes by tens of thousands were enlisted by
their emancipators. Thus, a small remnant fought
nearly the whole nation. In the progress of the
war, the North refused to exchange prisoners;
and, inasmuch as they had the most men, the
South suffered most from this barbarous policy,
compelling us to keep a large number of prisoners when we had hard work to feed our own men,
and then, forsooth, making the prisoners, whom
they held, responsible for the alleged privations of
the prisoners for whom they would not exchange.
The policy was to swap down on the part of the
strongest side. But this is a long story, and contemporary history is full of mutual criminations
and recriminations. The fact is, however, that
the records show more deaths proportionately
among the prisoners in Northern hands than
among those in our hands; and this is a sufficient
answer in the large to the charges of cruelty to
prisoners, which you will read of in Northern histories. But I must not dwell longer on this matter. A word, however, upon two points before
leaving this subject.

I spoke of the firing on Fort Sumter. Northern history expatiates on that fact, and iterates and reiterates the words, "The South fired the first gun." It sounds as if it had some meaning; but it is all sound, and signifies nothing. "Who was the aggressor? Who compelled the first gun to be fired? Who imperilled first the solemn compact between the States?" The whole antecedent history will fasten the blame elsewhere. If a man attacks me with gun in hand, and I shoot quicker than he does, it is true that I fired first; but, if he had not made the aggressive movement, there would have been no gun fired at all. The approach of the fleet to re-enforce Sumter ignited the match that fired the first gun. Another illustration. A boy puts a chip on his head, and dares another to knock it off. Instead of knocking the chip, suppose he knocks the head, which, if fighting be allowable, is the wisest policy. After the fight, the boy with the chip can say truly that the other hit the first blow. It is true; but, if he had hit the chip first, he would have received the first blow. But, when men are angry, nothing but fight will cool their blood; and fight they did, most lustily. History records no more gallant struggle under more gallant leaders than the South made. The issue being against us, multitudes changed their opinions, and said, "They must have been striving against right, or God would have given them the victory." But such reasoning cannot hold. It proves too much. Right, in the end and long future, will get its reward, but in ways and modes of God's own ordination, and not after man's measurements or upon men's small balances, which are not equal to judge and weigh such magnitudes as are involved in the divine plan with nations. I attempt to rescue a child that has fallen into the sea. I struggle manfully to save it, but I am drowned in making the attempt. It does not follow at all that I did wrong in making the effort to save the child. I would have failed much in duty if I had not made the effort. This is very plain, when applied to a small and familiar matter. It is equally true, if not equally plain, in the greatest matters. We fail to see it in great matters, because we cannot see far enough, and, particularly, because we estimate success by pitifully small standards. A man often saves his whole life by losing his physical, his present, life. Life must be estimated, not only by its *extent*, but by its *intent;* not only by its length, but by its breadth and depth. He who gives his life unselfishly for another, or for right or truth or honor, in the true sense of that word, has not lost, but has saved, his life. On the other hand, he who can look on, and see right and truth, or even a human life, threatened and imperilled, and make no effort to help, may, in a sense, have saved his life; but he has, in the deepest sense, lost it. He has already lived too long for his own good. This, now, my children, is an illustration, in the small, of great and eternal principles. Never measure duty or right by worldly and utilitarian standards. Some day, I hope, you will rejoice if you shall have to give your life a sacrifice to duty and truth. The life of our dear Lord was a great failure, tried by the worldly standards of His day. But where was there ever such a life, even upon principles of utility, when viewed in the large? When I think of the pure and noble-minded men who died on fields of battle for the South (and I withhold not my meed of recognition of like-minded men who were ranged on the other side), — men whom I knew and loved — Christian men, who gave themselves, life, and all, for what they deemed to be duty, — I cannot hope for any better portion than to be permitted to range myself by their side "on the other banks of the river."

DOMESTIC SLAVERY.

Now, a word about another matter that I briefly touched in a former page, — *Domestic Slavery!* It was the occasion of the war in a certain way, and it was done away with as one of the results of the war. The time will probably come when my descendants will look back, and wonder how their grandfathers could have held human beings in bondage.' I am concerned that they who come after me shall have some idea of the institution of slavery as it existed in Virginia; for I was more conversant with its character as displayed in the older States, where it was more patriarchal, less profitable, and in all respects milder, than in the South-western States, where absen-

---

[1] If it shall be regarded as an unpardonable offence to have held human beings in bondage, let it be borne in mind that it was an offence shared originally by all the United States.

There lies before me, as I write, a little newspaper (about eight by twelve inches in size) entitled

"THE NEW ENGLAND WEEKLY JOURNAL."
"MONDAY, April 8th, 1728."

In the column of advertisements of sermons, tracts, etc., I see the following:—

"☞ A very likely Negro Woman, who can do Household work, and is fit Either for Town or Country Service, about 22 Years of Age, to be sold. Inquire of the Printer hereof."

"☞ A Very Likely Negro Girl, about 13 or 14 Years of Age, speaks good English, has been in the Country some Years, to be sold. Inquire of the Printer hereof."

(Spelling and capitalization as in the paper.)

I have inserted the foregoing advertisements with the hope that they may serve as "conductors" to convey some of the lightning wrath of our Northern unfriends quietly and harmlessly to the ground. The Southern States would never have received cargoes of slaves but for Northern vessels, and Northern people kept them in bondage as long as it was profitable so to keep them. The philanthropy which sweeps away at a breath the wealth of other people, involves a very easy and cheap humanity.

tecism, that curse to the laborer, was more common. If you will read the allegations from the Northern side, and at all believe them as truly descriptive of slavery as it existed in the large, you will believe — to draw it mildly — a very large lie. That there were cases of oppression and violence and grievous wrong, is not to be doubted; for some men, in all countries and all ages, will be violent and oppressive — even to their wives and children. But because there have been cases where slaveholders have inflicted cruelty and wrong upon their slaves, it no more proves that cruelty was the characteristic of slaveholders, than it proves that men in the Northern States habitually maltreat their families, because, every now and then, some brute kicks to death a wife or child. People will be to their families — to their wives, children, and servants — what they are themselves. If kind and just in character, they will be just and kind to all around them. Then, superadd to this consideration the fact that men in the large consult their interests, and that it was greatly to their interest to treat their slaves well, and you have, besides the character of the owner, his clearest interest to treat well all his dependants. Slavery — like matrimony from the husband — takes its character from the master. If he be just and kind, his rule will partake of those characteristics. So with the father in his family, etc. As an illustration of a certain class of Northern ideas on this subject, — shortly after the war, I met with an honest-hearted man from the North. We fell, naturally, into conversation on the subject of domestic slavery. He asked me, "Is it true that in the South you were accustomed to hitch your negroes to the plough, and drive them?" He asked the question seriously. I asked him, "How many negroes would it take to draw a plough to any purpose?" — "Eight or ten, I calculate," said he. "Well," said I, "how much is a mule worth?" — "One hundred dollars," said he. "How much was a negro?" — "One thousand dollars," said he. "Well," said I, "do you think — to say nothing of our kind feelings towards our negroes — that we had no more sense than to use ten negroes, which were worth ten thousand dollars, to do a work which a mule, costing one hundred dollars, would do better?" — "Why," said he, "I never thought of that." — "Of course you didn't," I said: "there are many things of which you never thought on the same subject." The above is a pretty fair specimen of the notions of some ignorant and fanatical minds, many of which were wider still from the truth.

"UNCLE TOM'S CABIN."

There was a book, written by Mrs. Stowe,—a sister of the celebrated Henry Ward Beecher,—which had an immense circulation, and exerted a powerful influence. It was a work of fiction, entitled "Uncle Tom's Cabin." It was written with considerable ability, and was, in some respects, a most attractive and thrilling narrative. It collected together many incidents illustrative of the cruelty with which slaves were said to be treated in the South. They may have been true, or not true. You can find similar incidents in all the relations of life, in all ages, and among all people. Yet—strange to say—the book, if carefully analyzed, speaks volumes in favor of that which it was written to condemn. It was, essentially, a specimen of feminine logic. But let me explain. Shortly after the war I was in New York, and met with an old acquaintance. The conversation turned upon domestic slavery. I asked him how it was that the Northern mind had become so thoroughly abolitionized; telling him, that when I was a youth, pursuing my studies at old Yale, the abolitionists were few in number, and not of much social standing. He replied, that, in his judgment, "Uncle Tom's Cabin"—the book above referred to—had as much to do with the growth of a bitter feeling against slavery as any other agency, and asked me if I had ever read the book. "Of course I have," said I: "we all read it, and in some respects admire it — chiefly, its power as a work of fiction. If it pretends to describe slavery as it generally existed, it is pretty much a work of falsehood." "But yet," I continued to say, "very few have ever pondered that book, and extracted its truest and deepest meaning." — "As how?" said he. "In this way," I answered. "Tell me who was the most striking character in that book for honesty, fidelity, and piety?" — "Why, 'Uncle Tom,' of course," he said, — "one of the finest characters I ever read of!" — "Yes," I said, "he was; but who was Uncle Tom? Was he not a slave? and does not the book go to show, that, if you want to find the best specimen of honesty and piety among servants, you must seek him among the slaves? Africa did not produce him, does not now produce him. We think that domestic slavery tended to the production of just such a character; fostering the instinct of obedience, from which spring reverence and faith. Be this as it may, I can say this much without contradiction, — that, according to Mrs. Stowe's book, slavery is not *incompatible* with the highest development of honesty and piety in the slave." He pondered my remark for a moment, and said, "Of course, I must admit that much: it is so written in the book." — "Well, again," said I, "who was the most attractive character in the book?" — "Eva," he said, "one of the most lovely of her sex, gentle and refined, — a beautiful character indeed." — "Who was Eva? was she not a slaveholder?" — "Yes, she was." — "Then," I replied, "in so far forth as that book is concerned, if you want to find a specimen of a peculiarly gentle and refined young woman" (Eva was the young lady of the house in which Uncle Tom served), "you must seek for her among slaveholders. We have an idea that the relation between those two parties — the young mistress and the old servant — tended naturally to the production of the qualities described in them both. At any rate, you must admit, that, according to Mrs. Stowe, refinement in the woman is not incompatible with the position of ownership in slaves." — "Yes," he said, "I cannot but admit that much: it is so set down in Mrs. Stowe's book." — "And now, once more," I continued, "who was the worst character in the book?" — "Why, Legree," he answered, — "a vile and cruel man." — "Who was Legree? was he not a Northern man who came South, trafficked in slaves, and maltreated them?" — "That is all so," he answered. I then wound up the conversation by saying to my friend, "Then, the gist of the book is this: if you want a good, honest, and religious servant, seek him among the slaves — find an Uncle Tom; if you want to see a glorious specimen of womanly loveliness, seek her among the slaveholders — find an Eva: and keep every Down-Easter from having any power over the poor creatures. Mrs. Stowe's book must be held responsible for this conclusion." A profound silence ensued, and a profound silence should reign for a while among the chatterers on this subject. For all that was beautiful in that condition of society has passed away. And there was something beautiful in the relation between the parties — especially in the care taken of the young and the old. Beautiful and just and benignant was the patriarchal condition of slavery in the "Old Dominion." All gone, or going — the honest and loving-hearted Uncle Tom, the lovable Eva; fast going — the faithful old mammy, the decent and comely maid-servant, reverence, obedience, faithful service, and Uncle Tom piety — all vanishing into space; and what have we instead? Conflicts of races, animosity and distrust, jealousy of capital, suffrage without sense, religion without morals, service without reverence — Gog and Magog — the old war between oppressive capital and discontented labor — he that runs may read! I say this, without fear of just contradiction, that slavery, as it existed in my time, in the State of Virginia, — I say Virginia, for I was born and reared in that State, — presented the justest and fairest condition of society that I have ever seen or read of. The same was true, I doubt not, in other Southern States. Compare the condition of the slave laborer with that of any class of people in similar employment in other lands. Read of the condition of the manufacturing and laboring classes anywhere. The condition of the slave in the Old Dominion showed a larger remuneration for labor, and a kinder treatment, with a comfortable provision for old age. Alas! poor *old* black man now! I think I can say, with entire truth, that the large majority of slaves at Christmas Eve were well housed, well fed, well clothed, with something extra in the pocket. There were exceptions, of course, but inappreciable in a large view. Where is the parallel, in any country, among white laborers of same condition?

But when the issues of the war emancipated the black, and Republicanism clothed him with the rights of American citizenship, including that of suffrage, the South handed over to the country millions of people of African descent, prepared, in the judgment of a majority of the people of this country, to exercise the duties and enjoy the privileges of said citizenship. These were the "down-trodden slaves," so-called! What Christian mission has ever accomplished the same result on the coast of Africa? How is it with the Indians? If there be any truth in the coming histories of this country, such facts as these will not long be silent, but will speak in tones most eloquent of the benignant and civilizing power of domestic slavery. My heart warms even now as I recall the past, and there come up before me the memories of my childhood and early manhood; of the dear old mammy who took me into her arms, and made me sit in her lap, and eat of the buttermilk and the ash cake with apples in it, which with loving hands she had made ready for her "young master" when he came back from college. You, my children, who shall spend your lives in the Southern States, and shall take part in the effort to adjust the social and domestic life to this new order of things, will some day, I fear, be forced to appreciate what I have said of the past, and anticipate for the future. As yet, while I write these lines, we have some few of the old folks left. They have all of our love and respect. These have not yet learned to look distrustfully upon the friends of their childhood. Fond memories still bind them to their white friends. As to the young fry, who are not taught reverence and subordination, what is their destiny? I shudder to think of it. I hope that I may be mistaken. God knows that I am doing all in my power to avert the impending danger. But what can you hope for in the large, from a people, who, by their own confession, know little of the virtues of chastity and honesty? Would they come under the influence of a religion which makes "things which are true," "things which are honest," "things which are just," the foundation of their religious character, then we might hope to see a superstructure of "those things which are lovely and of good report."

But, alas! thrown off to themselves, — especially in our rural districts, where they outnumber the whites, — their religion oft becomes a caricature, not far short of the Fetichism of their native Africa.

The Church could help them, and is now putting forth more energy on their behalf; but alas! they cling to their own devices, and will have none of her ways.

We read and hear — *usque ad nauseam* — of the brutalizing and debasing effect of slavery upon the character of this people. All their degradation is referred to this relationship. Orators and pamphleteers expatiate upon the theme, until some people actually begin to believe there is something in it. But whence, and when, and through what period of time, came their present comparative advancement? It was not in Africa, nor from Africa, that the influence came which elevated him from the savage state. The white man goes to Africa, and has to write out a language for the natives. As a people, they have little inventive power. They seem to make slow, if any, advancement in their native land. Even under civilizing influences in their own country, they develop slowly and doubtfully. Yet, under the auspices of servitude in the Southern States, millions have been raised to American citizenship, which is denied to the ever-free Indian. If they were not fitted for it, what a shame to have given them power to dominate the white race, as they did in some localities! If they were so fitted, what a tribute to the elevating influences of Southern slavery!

And their citizenship was accomplished by a vote of a majority of the people of the United States!

I say nothing in vindication of slavery in its origin. It was a foul wrong, shared alike by North and South, and to be repented of by both sections with works meet for repentance. It was a foul wrong to sell Joseph into Egypt, and after-

wards to enslave his descendants there. Yet out
of this wrong the wonder-working providence of
God wrought good unto Israel. So may it be in
the case of Africa in America! I say nothing
regretfully of the fact — not the manner — of the
negro's emancipation. I am doing, as I have always
done, all in my power to help him in every manner. I am alike a debtor to the bond and the
free. But I do maintain, and that without fear of
reasonable contradiction, that the negro's present
civilized condition and capability is due to this
cause, — that he was brought closely into relations
with the white men — and the best white men —
in his state of servitude. The closer the relation,
— as in the family, — the more marked the advancement! Here is a fact which should be
deeply pondered by those who love and seek the
truth; viz., that the slaveholding population of
the Southern States were, for the most part, men
of standing and culture, imbued oftentimes with
a chivalry of spirit which forbade unkindness to
the slave who lived under his roof, who ate of
his bread, and hearkened unto his voice. A true
Southern man will not be unjust to his dog.

THE CHURCH QUESTION.

But I have to jot down some thoughts upon
higher and more enduring themes. The king-

doms of men come to an end: vast empires, that once swayed the destinies of the world, are known only on the pages of history. They rise, fall, and utterly come to naught. They are of the things of time, and perish with time. You, my children, will have a high duty to perform in being good citizens, in upholding law and the administration of law. It is a part of one's religion, as well as loyalty, to be law-abiding citizens. Our country, now peaceful after a bloody war, may continue so for years; but there are existing elements of conflict which will become explosive whenever the population becomes dense enough for ignition. The Old World is pouring in its tide of population — peoples of all religions and no religions — all jumbled in a mighty mass. What will come of it all, who can tell? One thing seems most certain, — that human affairs move forward, and not backward. The state of the world, at this writing, is doubtless better, on the whole, than at any former period of time, and there is no good reason for supposing that it will take a retrograde movement. You will have to adjust yourselves to the era in which you live, keeping a true manhood, whatever the issue. That will bring a man peace at the last: that makes the man.

But I must pass to the consideration of God's Kingdom — the Church of God. "*Of that king-*

dom," — as you have been taught to rehearse in the Nicene Creed, — "*there shall be no end!*" My great desire is that my children should have an inheritance in that Kingdom, and ever be associated with it as I and my fathers were. The whole matter, as you may easily suppose, has been my lifelong study, and I want you to have the benefit of my thoughts and conclusions thereupon. You will find the religious world much divided. I cannot speak of all the existing organizations, — for their name is Legion, — but I desire to put before you in a general way the attitude of that branch of the Church in which I have been reared, and of which you have been made members by baptism — the attitude, I say, of this Church towards the rest of Christendom. Its name is "The Protestant Episcopal Church," and it may be interesting to you to learn that this appellation was suggested by one of your ancestors. The name is not a felicitous one, but has a noble record and a roll of great men. This Church, as all your reading will show, is an offshoot of the Established Church in England, deriving its orders from that Church, also its Liturgy and usages. We must go a little back to inquire into the history of the Mother Church, before proceeding to outline the particular relation of her daughter to the religious world around it in this country.

CHURCH IN ENGLAND.

The Church of Christ was planted in England at a very early day — most probably by one of the apostles of our Lord. This you will find in any early history of the English Church. Representatives from the British Church were present at the councils of the Church at a very early day (A.D. 325), long before the unhappy division took place which separated the Eastern from the Western Church.

Rome, being the controlling power of the world for a long period of time, became, naturally, the centre of other influences, religious as well as political. The bishop of Rome, sustained by the civil and military power, had no great difficulty in obtaining ultimate recognition as the supreme ecclesiastical power in the west of Europe. England held out against her jurisdiction as long as possible, but finally acknowledged the supremacy of the bishop of Rome in things spiritual. Augustine, a missionary under Rome, went to England, and found the southern part of the kingdom — inhabited by the Saxon race — without the Christian faith. The British Church already existed when he put his foot on the coast of England. Little by little, in the course of time, the Church in England came under the domination of the

Pope. It went sorely against the spirit and temper of our English forefathers to acknowledge fealty to any foreign power, civil or ecclesiastical. They fought against it as long as possible, but had at last to yield. It was this spirit of jealousy against the intrusion of a foreign power, which made it so easy at a subsequent period to throw off the yoke which was to so many, even Romanists in doctrinal matters, a galling servitude. But a new era dawned. Books became multiplied, and knowledge was more generally diffused. The "Great Reformation" took place.

I must say a word about that great movement, of which all history of that age is so full. Henry VIII., the king of England at the time, was far from being a pattern of good morals. He was imperious and lustful. A decision of the reigning Pope of Rome crossed his purposes, and Henry asserted — as he had the right to do — the independence of the Church in England. The claim of the bishop of Rome, to exercise jurisdiction in England, had no divine, but simply a human, sanction. The yoke, therefore, was thrown off — as it had been put on — by human hands. It was a right and lawful thing done, although done by a bad man. This often happens. The wrath and the lust of men are often overruled to work out most gracious purposes. We are often twitted with the taunt that Henry VIII. was the founder of the English Church; whilst the fact is, that it existed centuries before Henry's day, and has existed centuries since. The same bishops exercised jurisdiction in England before and after the Reformation. There was no break in the line of Bishops whatever. The Church in England did not cease to be catholic because she then cast off many uncatholic doctrines and usages which had become incrusted upon her. Henry VIII. was ever a Roman Catholic in heart and doctrine. No prevailing doctrine was changed or modified during his reign. In fact, he won his title of "Defender of the Faith," for fighting Reformed Doctrines. God made use of his imperiousness and impatience of will to throw off a foreign yoke, which had been wrongly imposed and reluctantly worn by the great mass of English people. This emancipation set free the minds of men, and Henry's successors to the throne favored the mighty change which was being wrought in the religious mind; and thus it was, by little and little, as light and knowledge were vouchsafed, that the Church in England came out of the wilderness of superstition, cleansed from many corruptions, and stood forth, and now stands forth, the zealous maintainer of the Faith and Discipline "once delivered to the saints." Wherever her influence extends, light and knowledge are diffused, peoples are elevated, freedom is proclaimed, law is administered, and righteousness prevails. Take the map of the world. Look at the nations under Romish rule — Spain, Portugal, Italy, France, Ireland, and Mexico. What keeps these people in the background? What makes the difference in Ireland between Romanists and Protestants? Spain was ahead of England at the era of the Reformation. Englishmen studied in her schools of learning. But Spain extinguished the dawning light of the Reformation in the lurid glare of the Inquisition; and Spain has decayed from that day. The spirit of the Roman Church is calculated to undervalue the exercise of reason, and to arrest the spirit of inquiry, which has so stimulated scientific investigation, and made this age so fruitful in knowledge. Of course, this spirit may be carried too far, and may lead to mere rationalism. But what may not be carried too far? You cannot fertilize a spot of land without stimulating the growth of weeds, but you also cannot make the best kind of grain without fertilization. So, of the printing-press — it brings many bad thoughts to the mind, but it also brings the best thoughts out. It is a bad sign when any system or man avoids the light. "Let there be light," was the herald-cry in chaos, and chaos departed when the light came. The best test of the truth of any system, when you can make a large enough induction, is that furnished by our Lord, — "By their fruits ye shall know them." As a church influencing laws, literature, and morals, we do not fear to challenge Christendom. England is what she is, mainly through the Church in England; and, to this hour, she exerts a more enlightening and benignant influence upon the world than any other Nation. It will not do to turn from a large survey of her influence, and taunt her with being reformed by such a man as Henry VIII. She was deformed by that monarch. He was the foul spot that disfigured that era; but, as the rust, he ate away the chain that bound the Church to the court of Rome, and let her go free for her glorious mission of evangelization and civilization to the remotest islands of the sea. Flings at Henry, and twittings about his part in the Reformation, come with a bad grace from the Roman Church, which has preferred men to honor and to the highest places in her gift, — even the so-called chair of St. Peter (when it is doubtful whether the holy apostle ever sat in it), — men, I say, in comparison with whom Henry might be canonized as a saint. Read any history of the Popes (e.g., Ranke), and you will return to the pages of Henry's life with a sense of relief, bad as that life was. When you sum up all that the Church of England has done, in literature, in science, in learning, in works of beneficence, in sacredly preserving the word of God, in translating it for the peoples of the world, in disseminating the righteous principles of law and equity, in diffusing a spirit of freedom, and, with it, the needful checks and balances of government, we may well thank God for our English blood and traditions, and cherish them all as the priceless inheritance from our fathers, and at the same time, next to that imposed by the knowledge of salvation, the weightiest responsibility that rests upon us.

CHURCH IN AMERICA.

LET us come down a little in our review to the planting of the American colonies: chiefly from Great Britain they were planted. We see sometimes a spirit of rivalry and jealousy on the part of some American people towards the mother country, — a sentiment always unwholesome and ungracious, but peculiarly so when directed against our motherland. Our ancestors found nothing precious on these shores, save the land and the riches beneath it. That was a divine gift, and demands unspeakable gratitude. What else did they find? They brought with them their blood, lineage, language, laws, literature, and thousand-fold traditions, all of which moulded for them the new life and institutions in their newly found country. The wigwam of the Indian did not furnish forth the equipment with which our forefathers began the battle of life on the American continent. The principles of liberty and the knowledge of religion were not found here, but were brought here. The battle which settled the rights of men was fought on British soil, and won by our British ancestors. The particular form of government established here, after independence was secured, was the outgrowth of circumstances in large part; but the foundations and principles of our government were laid by statesmen who had drank deep at English fountains, and were trained in the traditions of English sires. Let it never be forgotten by my children, that the sons of Englishmen and of English churchmen were the great men — the giants — who fought the war of the Revolution, and laid the foundations of the American Republic. Time would fail me to enumerate them. Glance at the names of a few in the honored list, — Washington, Hamilton, Madison, Marshall, and a host of others — "*clara et venerabilia nomina.*" So it was in the unsuccessful conflict for Southern independence, — Davis, Lee, Johnston (Joseph E. and Albert Sidney), and an innumerable host of greater or lesser lights. Nor is this at all accidental. It comes by operation of a law, — the law of elective affinity. There is something of combined grandeur and simplicity in the spirit and services of the Church, which irresistibly, and oft unconsciously, draws to it such men (not raised in the Church) as Clay and Webster, for example. Besides, the training in the Church tends to the production of such men. The great men among the Methodists (such as Wesley and Whitefield, etc.) had Church mothers, and were early taught in the Church catechism, and baptized, confirmed, educated, and ordained in the Church.

HOW THE CHURCH WAS PLANTED IN AMERICA.

THE Church of England clergy (there being at that time no *Bishops* this side of the water) were ordained in England, and were under the jurisdiction of the English Church until the close of the Revolutionary war. You will find a full account of the whole matter in "Bishop White's (the first bishop of Pennsylvania) Memoirs." Bishop Seabury was consecrated Bishop of Connecticut by the bishops of the Church in Scotland. Bishop White of Pennsylvania, Madison of Virginia, and Provoost of New York, were consecrated by the bishops of the Church of England (the Archbishop of Canterbury acting as consecrator in his chapel at Lambeth). Thus the Apostolic succession was derived by this Church. Dioceses have sprung up through the whole land. Several of the States each comprehend at this writing, two or more Dioceses, the State of New York at this time five.

It is often asked, "How is it that this Church, claiming, as it does, the elements of a pure catholicity, should have failed to have gotten a stronger hold upon the great body of the people in this country?" The question is an important one, and demands a fuller answer than these "Reminiscences" seem to call for. If the failure referred to were the result of any want of adaptation on the part of this Church to meet the *needs* of the great mass of the people, it were a *fatal* defect. But it is not so. In the mother country, the poor equally with the rich meet at her altars. In the rural districts, prince and peasant receive together her teachings, and unite in her liturgy. The manufacturing-towns are the homes of Dissent. There the social jealousy and the impatience of subordination and the spirit of vulgar self-assertion most abound, and there Dissent is rife. The Roman Church has but little hold upon the native masses in this country, and she imports her poor. I refer to this fact because we are constantly taunted with the reproach of having no poor in our churches, and shallow people

— and most people are shallow — are made to think that the Church careth not for the poor. There is another view. Should the Church have so many poor? Should she not enlighten and elevate them? Should not the hovels of our laborers be made more comfortable, even if our churches were less gorgeous? Our system encourages giving to, and not taking from, the poor. Would not "our Father," who "careth for the poor," have it so?

I cannot suppress a very instructive incident. Passing once up the Alabama River, I fell into conversation with a gentleman of the Romish persuasion. After some talk, slightly sprinkled with controversy, he observed, "I do not think, sir, you can doubt that our Priests are more assiduous in the discharge of their duties than Protestant ministers are." — "I have not been struck with the fact, if it be a fact," I replied. "Now," said he, taking up a newspaper which he had been reading, "here is an account of a man who was hung near Philadelphia the other day. Who was on the scaffold with him, and giving him spiritual direction? None of your Protestant preachers, sir, — a priest, a Catholic priest." — "That's exactly where he ought to have been," I suggested. "Why, sir?" — "Because it was one of his flock that was to be hung. I have never myself refused to attend one of my flock to the scaffold, because I have not been called upon. The Church should save her sheep from such an ending." Let Peter pay pence to Ireland, and Ireland may not have to seek succor from America.[1] Protestant Irish seem to be thrifty. They cultivate potatoes rather than politics.

The situation of the Church in these United States is peculiar. Many of the old families — notably in New York, Maryland, and Virginia — were, as a matter of course, almost always (except in Maryland, where the Roman Catholic element was unusually large) Church families. In the wild settlements, there is always an undue jealousy of social distinctions on the part of the laboring class; and they prefer to congregate among those of their own order, where their means of living, mode of life, style of dress, and topics of thought and conversation, are more alike. As an instance: My first parish was along the banks of the James River, beginning about thirty miles above Richmond, and extending some fifty miles towards Lynchburg. The families attending my services at the beginning of my ministrations were almost exclusively from the class of wealthy planters. In the vicinity of my churches were Baptist and Methodist houses of worship, and there congregated the overseers and small farmers from the

[1] See note on page 294.

hill country. These people knew nothing of Church doctrine or order, but they wanted to associate with folk of their own condition and pursuits. The men wanted to gossip with their fellows, and their wives and daughters wanted their bonnets and gowns to be as good as their neighbors'. The effect of democratic institutions and the extension of suffrage and the abolishment of privileged orders was wonderfully rapid among the people of this country.

There is much discussion nowadays as to the question, "How to get hold of the masses." You can't do it at all by any system of operations of a mechanical character. There is a repulsion on their part, and produced by the very spirit of envy and jealousy and self-assertion which the Church tries to put down and eradicate. It can only result from a larger measure of that Divine influence which eradicates self, and inspires a thirst for truth. A minister, who himself is deeply imbued with the Divine gift, and has power and tact, can work wonders with this repelling prejudice, as he can with the other powers of darkness. And that is our only hope just now, — a faint one, I must confess. But, besides this indwelling spirit of social jealousy with its attendant ills, there were peculiar difficulties with which this Church had to contend in her earlier history in this country, —

difficulties which laid the foundation of sectism deep and broad. The clergy of this Church were, as a general rule, Englishmen. The Church itself went by the appellation of "*The English Church.*" We had no bishops and no seminaries — every thing was English. War with England filled the whole country with animosity against every thing "English" — church and state. A tide of odium and unreasonable hate went like a wave over the whole country, and threatened to ingulf all sacred memories that commonly attach men to the land of their forefathers. The Church suffered grievously for a long time, and has not to this day rallied from the shock received. The Clergy, many of whom were Englishmen by birth, returned to their native land, thus leaving many parishes vacant. Many of those who remained during the continuance of the Revolutionary war were incompetent, and, as is the case oftentimes with colonial ministers, were men of little character. A long interval ensued before bishops were set apart for America. The consequences of all this were disastrous in the extreme. Parishes went rapidly to decay; legislation confiscated church property, the gift of the crown or of English land-owners; popular prejudice ran fiercely against her institutions because they were stigmatized as "English." The masses of people became alienated. Methodism, then vigorous and aggressive, strongly appealed to the passions of the people. The landed gentry of the country still clung to the Church as the church of their fathers. They had intelligence sufficient to enable them to distinguish between the Church and the action of the British Government, which was so hateful to the colonists. But the zeal of the few remaining adherents to the Church was languid. They were uninstructed from Sunday to Sunday: they were rather disposed to fight for the Church than to live for it. With some few and striking exceptions, the state of things was as given here. You may judge of the low condition into which the Church had fallen from this fact, which I had from Bishop Meade of Virginia: He, in connection with my father (William H. Wilmer, D.D., afterward president of William and Mary), and one or two other earnest men, made united effort to revive the Church in Virginia. They first united in calling Bishop Moore to be their bishop. They took steps, also, to raise an endowment for a theological seminary, and carried it through. The theological seminary near Alexandria, Va., is the result of the effort then inaugurated, the instruction of students being first given in my father's house in Alexandria. Whilst going through Virginia soliciting funds for this object, Bishop

Meade (who was then a young man) applied, among others, to Judge Marshall (Chief Justice of the United States Supreme Court) for aid. The judge replied that of course he would not withhold his contribution. It was his church, and that of his forefathers, but he thought the idea of resuscitating it in Virginia was hopeless; and he expressed himself as full of regret that a young man of family and talent, as Bishop Meade was, should throw away his life in so quixotic an undertaking. "The *Old* Chief" (as Judge Marshall was familiarly called among his intimates) did not live to see the glorious future which has opened for the Church in Virginia from the dark and apparently hopeless condition in which he knew it. The clergy of Virginia can now be found in all countries of the world nearly. One of her sons is bishop of Japan: another was a bishop of Africa, and he succeeded a Virginian in that bishopric. Seventeen of her sons, born on her soil, are, or have been, bishops of dioceses in the United States.

But I have digressed. I started with the view of showing how it was that the Church in this country had so slender a hold of the masses. I said that it was not due to any lack of adaptation on her part to the needs of the more ignorant, but that it was occasioned by influences of another

kind, over which the Church had no control, and which she had no power to resist. In England, as I have said, the poor in the rural districts are devoted to the Church. I have seen them sitting in crowds, even upon the steps of the pulpit in rural churches. The fact is, that, the more ignorant a people are, the more they need the appliances for instruction which the Church affords. The liturgy, with its fulness and simplicity, and its rich provision of scriptural knowledge, is, if a luxury to the learned, a deep necessity to the unlearned. But all this the ignorant do not know; and they are so filled with prejudices by some of their teachers, who feed their pride and social jealousy, that they are almost inaccessible to the clergy of the Church. I have myself had some experience in this matter. My last work in Virginia was among the poor in the vicinity of Richmond. I was induced to take hold of the work by an intimate friend, —

JOHN STEWART OF VIRGINIA.

He was a big-hearted and big-brained man, a native of Rothesay, Scotland, — a man of wealth, acquired by his own intelligence and sagacity. We had been long intimate. In 1858[1] I received a letter from him in reference to the

[1] See Appendix for Letters.

poor in his neighborhood. He said that God had given him wealth, and he felt his responsibility for the right use of it; that it pained him to see his neighbors living in practical atheism; that, as for himself, he could go to Richmond to church, but these neighbors could not, or would not. He then proposed to me to undertake the work of a missionary among them, — offered to support me whilst thus engaged, also to build a church and all things properly appertaining thereto, etc. I did not at first take to the plan proposed. My ministerial life had been up to this time pretty much that of a missionary. I felt like settling down to the duties of an organized parish. I found no one scarcely who did not regard the scheme as chimerical. The outlook was not a cheerful one at all. But, to make a long story short, after thinking over the matter for some time (Mr. Stewart had asked me to ponder it, and, to use his own characteristic words, to "spread it, as King Hezekiah did, before the Lord"), I concluded at last to accept the offer, — he to pay and pray; I to teach and preach, not without prayer, I trust. Nobly did he redeem his every promise. I preached, and went from house to house. He prayed as I preached. I shall ever believe that his prayers were the prevailing power. As it was with the centurion of old, "his prayers and his alms went up for a memorial, and were had in remembrance before the Lord." I can see him now, with uplifted eye, moist with tears, praying as I preached. Rich blessings came down from above on our work. We began services in a schoolroom, the use of which we shared with the ministers of various communions. By little and little we gained the hearts of the people. They were gathered, high and low, to the altars of the Church. Very soon a church was built, nominally and to an inappreciable extent, by the people of the congregation, but really by Mr. Stewart and his brother Daniel, a worthy brother of his brother John. Then a parsonage was built, etc. At the conclusion of three years, or within a few weeks of that time, we had a full and earnest congregation. At that time (and I had consented to give at least three years to the work) I was elected Bishop of the Diocese of Alabama. I have jotted down these reminiscences for several reasons, — first, because it was an interesting and suggestive period of my life; second, because it records the piety and zealous conduct of a layman, showing what an earnest man can do, if he has the heart to work; thirdly, to show how the poor can be reached, and brought into the Church; and, lastly and chiefly, to pay my tribute to the truth and faithfulness of the Divine promise to answer prayer, and to bestow blessings whenever and wherever "prayers and alms" come up before God for a memorial. This, in my judgment, is the true way to reach the masses, ever to "*consider the poor.*" That means much more than to give a needy man an occasional alms. We must "condescend to men of low estate," and none of us are so high as to have to stoop very much to find ourselves on a level with the very poorest. I admitted a very poor man to the Church by baptism whilst I was minister of "Emmanuel Church," — the church which had been built by the Messrs. Stewart. When the poor fellow sought me out, I asked him what his motive was, and how he came to seek admission. He replied that he was very ignorant, and could not read, and did not know much about "church matters," as he called them; "but," said he, "I have noticed a great deal, and have always seen the ladies of your church caring for the poor, visiting the sick and afflicted, and teaching the children," etc.; "and I concluded that where such good fruit grew, the tree must be a good one." God bless our faithful women!

Well, I have brought you down to my period of middle life in my "Reminiscences," to the time when I was elected Bishop of Alabama. Before passing on, I will only remark that I have every reason to believe that my having taken what was thought to be a lowly position, turned out in the end to my advancement. I doubt very much whether I would ever have been thought of for the bishopric of Alabama, if I had not taken that position. The success of the undertaking, in answer to the prayers of my friend Stewart, was so marked as to draw attention to myself as the visible working-power. So it often is. A man rises by stooping. He seems to rise with a spring. Only do your duty, my children, as the leadings of Providence may indicate, and He will direct your paths. I learned that lesson first from my mother, and my whole life abounds with illustrations of its truth.

I must add something more to what I have written of my friend, John Stewart. I called him a "big-brained" and "big-hearted man." What I have written of him will show what a big heart he had; and if all the people whom he has helped with his charities were to subscribe to the publication of this memoir, it would cost the author nothing to publish it. His munificent gifts extended not only to kindred, friends, and neighbors in this country, but went back in a continuous refluent wave to his native land, Rothesay, Scotland.

I heard in the most incidental way — for he had the characteristic reticence of his countrymen in a marked degree — that he sent regular remittances to his superannuated pastor in Scotland, for the reason that the old man had taught him his catechism in childhood. More than this, he and his brothers, Daniel and Bryce Stewart, built at Rothesay, Scotland, "*The Norman Stewart Institute for the Moral and Intellectual Advancement of Workingmen,*" and endowed it for all time. This Institute was named after the uncle of the brothers Stewart, who had left them property, a part of which was thus consecrated to a work of charity, thus bringing to completion a design for which their uncle Norman had made a partial provision in his will. In this way the works of large-hearted men do follow them through all time, and thus may men become "like their Father in heaven," and cause "their very paths to drop fatness." His large heart and mind find beautiful expression in his last will and testament. I had always expected that he would leave some considerable amount, either to found or sustain some benevolent or religious institution. When I ascertained that he had not done so, I felt some surprise and disappointment. But he had larger views than I had ever attained unto, and gave me an idea altogether new. One of the chief pleasures of his life had been to bless others with his wealth. He wished his wife and children to enjoy the same pleasure with himself, and he knew them well enough to know that what had been his pleasure would be theirs also. In this spirit he framed his will, an extract from which brings out his whole thought, as exquisitely beautiful as it is original. I bring it out here to illustrate the man and to perpetuate the sentiment.

Extract from John Stewart's will: —

"I have made no bequests to charitable or religious institutions, partly because what I might thus give would belong to my wife and children, but chiefly because I wish to impress on their minds the duty, the privilege, and the sweetness, of their giving from right motives, — that is, for Christ's sake, while they are yet alive."

Most nobly have they justified his faith in them.

I have seen a great many people who were "willing to communicate:" he exemplified the rare instance of one who was "glad to distribute." More than once, when we were building together a house for the Lord, and I would come to him for help in succoring the distressed, — he had asked me to be his almoner, — has he handed me the amount needed with his eyes moistened with tears, and the words, "I thank you for giving me this opportunity." What luxuries the rich deprive themselves of by not blessing others, and how poor they are amid all their extravagance! The inmate of an almshouse need not envy the millionnaire who is "rich toward himself, and poor toward God."

St. Xavier has left on record a marvellous statement, — "I have had"—I think he stated more than a million — "many people resort to me for confession. The confession of every sin that I have ever known or heard of, and of sins so foul that I never dreamed of, has been poured into my ear, but no one person has ever confessed to me the sin of covetousness!"

Yet this sin is the "root of all evil" in the sight of Heaven. I can give almost the same experience with St. Xavier. One man only has ever expressed to me the fear lest he should become covetous; and it is a suggestive fact, that he was the most generous man that I have ever known, — John Stewart. We used to talk this matter over frequently. He would say, "I have noticed that covetousness is the prevailing disease of old people; I fear it for myself as I get older; and I know of but one remedy, — giving! giving! giving!" He had hit both the diagnosis and the treatment of the disease. The spring will become stagnant unless its waters flow freely : the embankments of the dam will give way unless there is a "waste" to carry off the excess of water. Is it not a suggestive fact, that the most liberal are the most fearful of selfishness? It is natural that it should be so. The most learned feel most their ignorance; the most humble their pride; the most pure their uncleanness; and for the same reason, the most generous their selfishness. He who habitually walks in the "light of God's countenance" sees all the little motes and atoms of remaining imperfection, from which he would fain cleanse himself. The concentrated light of the sun through the solar microscope discloses to view, in the seemingly pure drop of water, most horrid forms of living beings. It is not cant, then, but a clear vision and an humbled spirit, that brings out from the holiest saints confessions of sin, and cries for cleansing.

I have written of the heart of my friend: a word now about his mind, which was as broad and all-embracing as his heart. I cared not to read books much, when we were in daily intercourse. His book was the Word of God; and for his knowledge of that Word, I pay high honor to his Scotch Presbyterian training. The Bible was his daily companion and his daily food. No subject could be brought up that he did not illuminate and illustrate by Scripture quotations and allusions. He was not a great talker, but always spoke to the purpose when he did talk. In company, after a subject had been pretty much talked out, he would, usually, in some one or two pregnant sentences, settle the matter by a generalization which brought out the principles of the whole subject under discussion. This power of generalization is the attribute of a great intellect. To such a mind, there is no isolated fact : it takes its place in the great system of phenomena as the example and illustration of a general principle or law. John Stewart talked very much as Lord Bacon wrote.

We were together every day, and many hours in the day, whilst the war of the States was brewing. Living within a few miles of Richmond, and going to the city daily in his company, I had the benefit of his large and comprehensive views, especially upon the financial aspect of the whole question. What all men now see, he saw then, and with perfect distinctness. His prophecy has become literal history. What perplexed others, was as plain as the day to his mind.

Withal, there was in the play of his mind, as is common with such minds, a delicate humor and wit, which, when argument had not convinced, would end the whole discussion. I wish now that I had treasured up some of his sayings which were at that time so current among his intimates, but they have faded from my memory. There was not only point in them, but, usually, a deep moral. One only comes into my mind at this time, and it is but one of thousands of like character. "Stewart," said a Richmond friend, "I am coming out to dine with you some Sunday: it's the only day that I have to myself." — "That's unfortunate," was the reply, "for that is the only day that is not mine own. I have had given me six days in the week all to myself, to 'do what I have to do:' the day you mention is the Lord's day. My great desire is to dedicate its hours to Him whose day it is."

This brings me to speak of his piety. That was his crowning and all-covering grace. He never mentioned the name of Deity save with hushed utterance. A holy awe seemed to come over his face, and tremble in his voice, when the Divine Majesty was named by him. I seemed to feel the Divine Presence when he mentioned that Holy Name. Then, too, his faith was so childlike. All great men have such faith. I remember when Judge John Cochran of Eufaula, Ala., came to talk with me about his own confirmation, I could not but contrast his speech with that of some very smart men who have talked with me on the same subject. I asked him about his "faith," which he would have to profess in confirmation.

I can never forget his childlike look when he answered, "I have implicit faith in God's holy Word as summed up in the Catholic Creed: I never try my reason in matters beyond its grasp. My Father has spoken to me through His Son: I believe." Cochran had the largest mind that I have yet met with in Alabama. The first time I ever saw him was made notable by an incident quite characteristic of the man. We met on the road — I going to his house, and he going to see me. As we met, a friend, who was driving my carriage, called out, "Judge, this is the bishop." The judge was absorbed in a large book, and incontinently sprang from his seat into the road, tumbling the book into the sand, and warmly welcoming me to the neighborhood. The book was Shakspeare. That and the Bible were his constant study. There was no danger of being sceptical with such daily companionship. Great minds are never sceptical. Dear Judge, you, too, have passed away, and one light more has gone out from my life.

But I have strayed from my subject. I could not let that dear friend Cochran be left out of my "Reminiscences."

I was speaking of my friend Stewart's piety and reverence. I cannot take the veil from his family circle, and show him there as he was, husband, father, brother, and friend. He is still there, sanctified with all holy memories; and the memory of his words and life still keep burning the sacred fire.

I said he was brought up in Scotland. He was, therefore, as was to be expected, baptized in the Church of Scotland. For that Church he never lost his love and reverence. I should have esteemed him less if he had. But his deepest religious impressions were received during that wonderful revival — *that was indeed a revival* — that went like the breath of heaven over Virginia nearly fifty years ago, when he received confirmation. There was a wonderful attraction for his mind and heart in the grand liturgy of the Church, that same liturgy for which some of the best minds of the Presbyterian Church in Scotland and America do now yearn; and no son of the Church ever appreciated her holy services more than he did. He often said to me that "the ways of the Episcopal Church in this country were more like those of the 'Free Church' of Scotland than any other, and he felt more at home in her services."

I used to banter him about his "Churchmanship," etc., although he was worth a score of our ordinary Churchmen, and tell him that I did not expect to make much of a Churchman out of such

Scotch material as he was made of, but that I was thankful to have him just as he was. I remember now sending him a published sermon of mine on "The Church of the Living God, the Pillar and Ground of the Truth," saying to him that I did not expect him to fall in with some of the views expressed. His reply was quite characteristic, and has ever since been suggestive. Many of our Churchmen might ponder it to advantage. "You cannot put the Church too high for me, if you always keep the Head above the body." That is a fair sample of his manner of speech and writing.

Many friends who have sojourned at "Brook Hill," Mr. Stewart's residence near Richmond, and have been privileged to worship at the family altar, a sacred shrine in that household, have told me of the singular impressiveness of the whole scene at family prayer. I have always regretted that I could not have enjoyed that privilege, my ministerial office calling upon me to officiate myself when present. They have told me that an inexpressible solemnity attended those services. The deep utterance of the father's voice, and profound awe, the simple and grand language of address before the throne, all made them feel that God was in the midst of them.

I named a son after him, John Stewart Wilmer, a dear, blue-eyed little fellow, who was soon taken home. What remains of him on earth lies hard by the walls of dear "Emmanuel," the church which his godfather Stewart and I had together builded. Near by — and I love to think that together they will rise at the last day — lies what was mortal of his namesake. "Emmanuel" (God with us) Church seems to guard the precious spot.

I have named for him now a grandson, John Stewart Jones, another blue-eyed boy. I ask no more for him from Heaven than that he may have a portion of the mind and heart that dwelt in his namesake, John Stewart.

In the sketch here given of my dear friend Stewart, I may, perhaps, have left an impression that he was a stern man. He was a stern man, — stern as granite in his convictions of truth and duty. Neither fear, favor, nor affection could move him a hair-breadth in such matters; for he lived habitually in the light of the Divine Presence, and the judgment of man had no weight when his conscience had decided. His character in this respect is strikingly brought out in the inscription upon his tombstone, "Blessed is the man whose strength is in Thee, in whose heart are Thy ways."

To the casual acquaintance he ordinarily appeared to be a very grave man; and friends whom I have introduced to him have often asked me,

"Is not your friend Mr. Stewart a very austere man?" a question which always amused me, who knew him in his family privacy and inner life. Ah, how genial and bright he was here in his home-circle and among his intimates, where the warm beams of his loving nature, and the bright sparklings of his refined humor and wit, made a very sunshine in his dwelling!

His heart was as full of thanksgiving as of supplication. More than almost any one I ever knew, he illustrated in his every-day life the injunction of the holy apostle to "be careful for nothing, but in every thing, by prayer and supplication with thanksgiving, let your requests be made known unto God," etc. Hence came the habitual peace which pervaded his heart, and irradiated his dwelling.

As a father, he was so loving, so tender, so considerate, so mindful of human infirmity, that his dear children will ever be able to reproduce from the remembrance of the earthly father refreshing and comforting views of the Divine Father. Thus did he let his light so shine in his household that all around him — children, servants, and friends — saw his good works, and glorified their Father which is in heaven.

He has passed out of mortal sight; but long will the radiance of his bright and holy life shine upon his dwelling-place, even as the light of parting day lingers upon the horizon long after the sun has gone down.

He made unto himself "friends of the mammon of unrighteousness." He builded God a house. Shall he not enter into everlasting habitations? May my end be like his, and my habitation with him forevermore!

DIFFERENT RELIGIOUS BODIES IN THE UNITED STATES.

Now I desire to say something about the different religious bodies with which you will come in contact, and to point out their characteristics and claims, and to show you your relation to them. It is most important that you understand these things, — first, that you may give an intelligent reason for your own position in Christendom, and also be prepared to instruct others in matters of so great concernment. That there should be divisions among Christian people, is much to be deplored for every reason. Division runs counter to the mind of our Lord, whose prayer ever was, "Father, that they may be one as We are one." Again, it breeds unholy contention and emulation; divides forces, and wastes energies; practically, it divides to a certain extent (and it is to that extent injurious) the Kingdom of God against itself. The divided state of Christendom is gloried over in a certain kind of flash oratory, which describes the varied hues of a divided Christianity as a beautiful kaleidoscopic picture, where are displayed all the prismatic hues of light — forgetting that where the colors of the prism are exhibited, it is in consequence of refraction, and does not present the pure light as it comes from heaven. Or, as some others delight to view it, they describe the various denominations as regiments or divisions of the grand army, fighting under one Captain, — the great Captain of salvation. All this sounds very pretty, and is sufficiently captivating to a certain sort of mind; but the lamentable fact is, that these several regiments or divisions — call them what you will — are spending a large part of their strength and time in fighting and firing into each other. They have to keep three or four ministers in a little village (where the services of one good man would be sufficient), to watch each other, and keep the balance of power even. At this moment two-thirds of the ministers in the villages might be sent to the heathen, to the great advantage of Christendom. Time would fail me to enter into all the evils of schism. Yet we find good and true men among all the great denominations. We must not ignore that fact, nor that other great fact, — that this goodness which we see is the fruit of the Divine Spirit, and the outcome of union with Christ. They could not else manifest, as they do often, the fruits of the Spirit. These are the actual phenomena with which we have to deal, — to deal fairly and honestly. Hence we are called upon to distinguish between men and their systems and organizations. The latter may be a mistake, a wrong, an injury; and yet, through the frailty of sinful men, good men may be earnestly, however mistakenly, working under them. With some men it is a lust of power, an ambitious spirit, a desire to exalt self. Divisions ordinarily spring from unruled lusts of ambitious men, good men, too, it may be, but not good enough to kill their ambition. With some other men, their denominational connections are the result of ignorance and shallowness: they really think they are promoting the purity of the Church by a wholesome rivalry. With the great mass of men, it is a matter of accident or of pure indifference. They don't care or think much about the matter. Now, I hold — and have ever taught, both publicly and privately — that the divided state of Christendom is an evil of incalculable magnitude, and that it becomes every Christian man to do what in him lies to heal the breach. He cannot do it, in my judgment, by treating the evil lightly, nor by contention and strife. The evil comes from the Evil One: the counteracting good must come from the Author and Giver of all goodness. All work for whatever good end, if not done in the spirit of Christ, intensifies the evil sought to be remedied. It adds fuel to the fire: it feeds, instead of quenching, the flame. I hold — and have ever taught and preached it — that each Christian man should, so far as his intelligence goes, seek to know what is the truth in all this matter of a divided Christendom. The very spirit and desire to find out the truth is a good beginning, and will not end there in any earnest mind. The difficulty would not long exist were men earnestly to go to work to find out the truth, with the love of the truth to inspire their search. One has no business to talk about any truth in any other spirit, no more than he would have a right to talk about the properties of angles, etc., unless he had learned something of geometry. The good in an evil thing is often only apparent on the surface: the evil often poisons and corrupts the whole system.

But I am dwelling too long upon these generalities. I must come to a nearer and more tangible view of the subject, only observing, at the outset, that every man, and every body of men, should give an account of themselves, when they came into being, and what good purpose they are subserving by continuance in being; in a word, the "*raison d'être.*" I take up, first, the

ROMAN, OR LATIN, CHURCH.

I TAKE this Church first, because she is the largest Christian organization in the world; and, furthermore, she claims to be the only legitimate, divinely appointed communion of Christians on earth. You will meet the claims of Rome everywhere, in books, newspapers, schools, colleges, etc. A wonderful piece of mechanism it is, a vast, complex, flexible and inflexible power, suited to all temperaments, adjusting itself to all idiosyncrasies, and, as it regards the great "Society of Jesus" especially, politic, daring, or submissive, as the case may call for, to the last degree — alas! in what painful contrast with the simplicity of "the truth as it is in Jesus." Rome is to-day pretty much what Jesuitism is; because Jesuitism, after having fought the world, and even the Bishops of Rome sometimes, and after having been expelled in turn from nearly all the countries of Europe, has achieved its present commanding position, gives counsel to popes, causes doctrines to be promulgated, — new doctrines upon the same platform with the ancient Creeds. Rome *claims to be exclusively "the Catholic* Church." The Church in

England, as I have before written, was at one time under the jurisdiction of the Bishop of Rome; so were all the churches of Western Europe. The Church in England is not now; but Rome, none the less, asserts her claim, and promulgates decrees and dogmas as by divine warranty. Within my memory, she has taken a private opinion of individuals, and elevated it to the dignity of a fundamental dogma, — "*the immaculate conception of the Blessed Virgin.*" Later still, and in my day, she has promulgated the dogma of the "*infallibility of the Pope,*" — has done it formally; and her adherents, some of them reluctant, and some recalcitrant for a while, have either formally given in, or preserve a still silence. Strange — and yet not strange — it is, that the promulgation of infallibility synchronized exactly with the passing away of all her temporal dominion. This fact is exquisitely brought out by Mozley in his "University Sermons." I cannot forbear a single extract. He is speaking of the proclamation of infallibility by the Pope at the moment of his stepping down from the throne of temporal dominion. "Is this not," says Mozley, "the act of a dispossessed monarch, who, upon the eve of the crisis, collects all his greatness about him, and prepares to quit his throne with a rigorous statement of his rights first put forth? . . . The claim represents former possession. Rome issues out of her own gates, taking her history with her; she collects her prestige, she gathers up the past, she calls in all the antecedents of her temporal greatness; she stereotypes memory in decrees; she condenses history into dogmas; she surrounds herself symbolically with all the insignia of her secular glory. . . . A thousand banners and escutcheons are hid in one of those sentences which makes the *statement* of her dominion, in order to serve as a support to her in the loss of the *fact*. . . . All in vain! The earth must roll back on its axis before the moral sense of society recants on these questions. . . . Never again, never, though ages pass away, never any more under the heavens, shall be seen forms and fabrics and structures and combinations that we have seen. They have taken their place among departed shapes and organisms, deposited in that vast mausoleum which receives, sooner or later, all human creations. The mould in which they were made is broken, and their successors will be casts from a new mould. The world is evidently at the end of one era, and is entering upon another; but there will remain the Christian creed and the Christian Church, to enlighten ignorance, to fight with sin, and to conduct man to eternity" (pp. 22-24 of Mozley's "University Sermons").

Upon what grounds, you may well ask, does

Rome build her vast pretensions? Chiefly upon a declaration of our Lord to St. Peter: "Upon this rock I will build My church," etc. If the words mean what the Romanists affirm they do mean, there is no declaration that they confer any special authority or privilege upon the Bishops of Rome. For, in the first place, it is a mooted point whether St. Peter was ever Bishop of Rome. St. Paul certainly was there, and also wrote the "Epistle to the Romans." But, besides, you must interpret the meaning of our Lord's declaration in the light of subsequent history. Is there any evidence to show that St. Peter claimed the pre-eminence said to have been conferred upon him in these quoted words, or that it was ever conceded to him by the other Apostles? The contrary is the fact. Rome is not the "mother" of churches. Jerusalem, where the Christian dispensation of the Church was inaugurated, is the mother church. And you will observe that at the meeting of the first council of the Church (Acts xv.), St. James, the first Bishop of Jerusalem, was the presiding Bishop; St. Peter merely giving his opinion as a member of the council. St. Peter gave his *opinion*, whereas St. James concluded the deliberations of the council by saying, "*Wherefore my sentence is*," thus announcing the judgment of that body. How can such a state of things be accounted

for from the Romanists' position in regard to
the so-called successors of St. Peter? It was
many years before a Bishop of Rome claimed
any thing like supremacy; and her claim was never
recognized by the Church Universal. The Oriental churches never fell under the power of the
Bishop of Rome. They exist to-day, and have existed from the beginning, apart from the sway of
the Bishop of Rome. It is the most shameless
and groundless assumption, that of the claim
of the Pope to universal supremacy and — as a
corollary therefrom — to infallibility. When you
read, as you will, in history of the counter-decisions
of bishops of Rome, and of the profligate lives of
many of them (history records no worse characters
than some of them), it is almost amusing, were the
consequences less serious, to hear such announcements as are made of the power of the Pope.
Flings at the English Church, because of *Henry
VIII.'s* character, come with a bad grace from men
who now, as a matter of salvation, must believe in
the infallibility of a *Borgia!* Then, too, when
you come to the matter of doctrine, — that of
transubstantiation, the worship of the Blessed
Virgin, the Romish purgatory, etc., — you, who
have been instructed in the word of God, can
hardly be drawn away from the ancient faith into
the mazes of Romish error. The best antidote

against all uncatholic doctrine is a thorough acquaintance with the Word of God, as interpreted and accepted by the Universal Church. It is a two-edged sword, that guards in all directions the tree of life. Make it, my children, your book of counsel, the guide for time and eternity, health for body and soul. Yet, think not that I join in the popular and undiscriminating tirade against Rome. She has the faith, though sadly disfigured, and enrolls among her children a goodly fellowship of saints and a noble army of martyrs, — not, indeed, because of her errors, but in spite of them. In many things, we might imitate the zeal and spirit of self-sacrifice so wonderfully illustrated in her communion. Roman-Catholicism, in so far as it is true to the catholic faith, is one thing, and worthy of all admiration. But Romanism, as corrupted by *new* doctrines, and perverted by Jesuitism, which just now is in the ascendent, and dictates, as is thought, the policy of that Church, is quite another thing. Against all these uncatholic features of the Roman Church, this Church of ours enters her solemn protest. Hence, she is called the *"Protestant"* Church, because she is so truly *catholic.* Her Protestantism constitutes really the negative side of her Catholicity. We do not believe in "The Protestant Episcopal Church." And why? Because our faith cannot properly rest in any one branch of the

Church. Any particular church may err in the faith. Rome assuredly has; she has erred by unwarranted additions to the faith; she imposes uncatholic conditions of communion and fellowship. We cannot fraternize with her, without accepting as true what is not true. Besides, she has excommunicated us: we have never excommunicated her. The schism between us is not of our making. We are ready to meet her, and all the historical churches (by this I mean all churches tracing an Apostolic succession of the ministry), upon the basis of catholic truth,—that which always was everywhere, and held by all,—our faith being in the Holy Catholic Church, and only using the appellation of "*Protestant Episcopal*" by way of designating a branch of the Church, and because it has a well-known doctrinal and historical significance; just as we designate continents and oceans and bays and rivers, to localize and designate them, but not to deny or lose sight of the fact that all these several divisions make up the great land and sea.

"*Pray for the peace of Jerusalem.*"

THE PRESBYTERIAN COMMUNION

Is a select, learned, and most respectable communion of Christian people. Why is it called *Presbyterian?* To indicate the fact that their ministers are presbyters merely, and that they recognize no office in the Church like that of our Bishops. That Denomination has precedence in Scotland, an existence in England and Ireland, in France and the United States, besides scattered congregations on the Continent, and missions among the heathen. Its history dates back no farther than the Reformation. There is no satisfactory record of a church up to that era which was not ruled by Bishops. They claim that their ministerial government was instituted by the Apostles, but admit that it soon merged into the Episcopal form. It will strike any one as very strange that the Apostolic form of government (supposing, for the sake of argument, that such was Presbyterian) should have lasted so short a time. There must have been a strong tendency to Episcopacy in early Presbyterianism. During the apostolic era, the Church was without controversy, governed by the Apostles. The first clear intimations of subsequent history give us Episcopal churches everywhere. If any change ever took place from Presbyterian to Episcopal polity, as they allege, history does not record the fact nor the time. The truth is, that all this talk is purely conjectural, imaginary, and hardly reasonable. If there is any truth in it, the burden of proof (positive) rests upon themselves. The whole stream of history is against the assertion. The analogy of nature, in its manifold headship, is against it. It is an afterthought altogether. Some of the most learned of their reformers — notably, Calvin — acknowledged the fact of primitive Episcopacy, and he would have ingrafted the feature upon his system had it been practicable.

The history of Puritanism in England is a most suggestive one. It originated in a certain school of divines in the Church in England who were enamoured of a more simple ritual than that of the Church, and held stronger views of the doctrines of predestination and election, etc., than "The Thirty-nine Articles of Religion" justified. The body of divines holding said views, at last, after many attempts had been made to pacify and harmonize them, went to themselves, established their standard, — "The *Confession of Faith*," — and thus took a determinate departure from the historical Church in England and other countries. They seemed to run counter to every distinctive feature of the Church: — we kneeled, they stood, in prayer; we kneeled at the Holy Eucharist, they sat and partook; they objected to the use of the surplice, to the sign of the cross in baptism, to the wedding-ring, etc. So trivial were the grounds of their dissent, as you will see in any history of the times. But times are changed; and they have changed, as we all have changed, with the times. No more do we hear of the peculiar doctrines of Presbyterianism. The great Fatherhood of God, loving all His children, and shining like the sun on all His creatures, has relegated to the tombs all those narrow, harsh, repelling, and appalling views of the Deity which came once from Presbyterian pulpits. They still sing, "Hark from the tombs," but the voice of the Easter-tide will drown that doleful cry after a while. Some of their best men are beginning to cry aloud for a liturgical worship. After a while they will demand it. Their sabbaths (Judaical as theirs have been) will give way to the "Lord's Day;" and they will sing Te Deums and Glorias, as other Christian people have done and will continue to do. Why they keep up their distinctive organization, it would be hard to say. What great truth they maintain distinctively, cannot be pointed out. What special attraction there is in their mode of worship, does not appear. They hold a great deal that is good, but they do not specially hold any thing good that the historical Episcopal Church does not also hold. You may say indeed, with truth, that distinctive Presbyterianism no longer exists, save in its ministerial polity; and that cannot stand the test of history. Chillingworth (in his "Apostolical Institution of Episcopacy Demonstrated") puts the allegation, on the part of the Presbyterians, that "Presbyterianism was ancient and Apostolic, but had run into Episcopacy" in a helpless condition. He says (p. 509), "When I shall see, therefore, all the fables in the 'Metamorphoses' acted, and prove true stories; when I shall see all the Democracies and Aristocracies in the world lie down and sleep, and awake into Monarchies, — then will I begin to believe that Presbyterial government, having continued in the Church during the apostles' times, should presently after (against the apostles' doctrine and the will of Christ) be whirled about like a scene in a mask, and transformed into Episcopacy. In the mean time, while things remain thus incredible, and in human reason impossible, I hope I shall have leave to conclude thus : 'Episcopal government is acknowledged to have been universally received in the Church presently after the Apostles' times.' 'Between the Apostles' and this "presently after," there was not time enough for, nor possibility of, so great an alteration.'

"And, therefore, there was no such alteration as is pretended. And therefore Episcopacy, being confessed to be so ancient and catholic, must be granted also to be Apostolic. *Quod erat demonstrandum.*"

The fact is, that Romanism and Presbyterianism, in some of their distinctive characteristics, are both uncatholic. They have more things in common than would be supposed at a first glance. They both ignore and undervalue patristic learning and authority. Presbyterian ministers, although well educated in the general, are proverbially deficient in patristic lore. They find no comfort in reading the "Fathers," for they ever find Episcopacy, and Episcopacy is most unsavory to them. The Romanists, likewise, run away from the Fathers nowadays. They are always seeking for proofs of the Pope's supremacy, and the Fathers did not know any thing about so novel a doctrine. The English Church with her weighty artillery has driven the Romish controversialists out of their old intrenchments, and they are now seeking a new position of defence in the doctrine of "development," which, as practically interpreted by them, means, not development of truth revealed, but revelation of new truth. Newman and Manning have both helped them on this new line. The only safety is in Catholic truth, and in the Apostolical order of the Church, which comes to us with the same universality of evidence that the Holy Scriptures themselves do, —*catholic consent*. And he who disparages the idea of *catholic consent*, disparages the very foundation upon which the Canon of Holy Scripture rests for its authenticity.

But the vital matter for men to know amid all these controversies is this, — that spiritual life comes from the indwelling of the Divine Spirit, the Lord and Giver of life. He dwells in men, despite many opposing infirmities, errors, and sins, else would He not dwell in any one of us. How far a man may go in error or sin without quenching the life of the soul, is not revealed. We may not expect in this our earthly pilgrimage to live without these clogging errors and faults, but let it be our aim really to *live*. It matters little what a dead man believes, — there is not much difference in dead things: they are all putting on corruption. But there is, on the contrary, a vast difference in living things. The nearer one lives in the truth and to the truth, the more of a man is he, and the higher his possible usefulness and destiny. Therefore, my children, strive to walk in the truth, and with boundless compassion for the ignorant and erring — not difficult for any one to do who fully realizes his own frailty and fallibility.

But we must say a few words about our

BAPTIST FRIENDS.

They are a very large denomination in this country, but do not exercise the same power with the Methodists, because they lack compactness and unity in their organization. They sprang up about the time of the Lutheran Reformation; and in some places they were turbulent and very heady, as Luther testified. In their Polity, they are Independents and Congregationalists; each congregation containing within itself governmental powers — each congregation an autonomy. They form among themselves what they style "*Associations;*" but these are purely voluntary, and are clothed with very limited powers.

Their boast is, that they possess "no written creed:" they do not baptize children, and they regard immersion as the only valid baptism, — indeed, as alone baptism. They ignore the question of the ministry pretty much, and attach a supreme importance to two things, — no children baptized, and adult believers alone to be baptized, and by immersion. They have among them some quite distinguished and learned men; but as a denomination, viewed in the large, their preachers and people are much less informed than the majority of the other sects. Of late they are earnest promoters of education. They are exclusive, — would be called very High Church among us, — but by their fraternizations with other Christian people in preachings, etc., they get credit among the unthinking for a liberality which is not deserved; for they will not commune with their fellow-

Christians, and they will repel them from their communion-tables. The Holy Scriptures they profess to take as their sole guide, and ignore all idea of the Catholic Church as an interpreter of divine truth. Hence, they have no written creed, and glory in the fact, although they hold certain opinions as unquestionably true; and it is hard for any one to see what is the difference between a *spoken* and a *written* creed. The creed of every man is what he believes to be true; and whether he writes it down, or lets it float in speech, it is none the less a creed, although, being unwritten and unrehearsed, it is liable to easy change. What idea can you form of one's faith, when he says, "I believe in the Holy Scriptures"? The arguments of the Baptists are plausible to a certain extent among the ignorant; and they beguile — not to deny much knowledge among their learned men — a great multitude of ignorant and really good people.

I cannot pretend to go at length into the matters of difference between us and them. There are a great many good and satisfactory books, which, if you should ever happen to need, you can consult. Among them I name one, written by Dr. Hodges, an old friend of mine, entitled, "Baptism, tested by Scripture and History," an argument, in my judgment, unanswerable. I merely touch a few points.

INFANT BAPTISM.

They reject *infant* baptism, alleging two principal objections: (*a*) the Scriptures do not in so many words command children to be baptized, and (*b*) that children are incapable of receiving any benefit therefrom. Whereas, on the contrary (as you will see more at length in the book referred to), children are always treated of in Scripture as belonging to the Church. They were circumcised into it under the Jewish dispensation; and when families and households were brought into the Christian fold, they were baptized as "households." Furthermore, our Lord gave it as a reason why His disciples should not bar the approach of children to Himself, that "of such is the Kingdom of God," which is the Church of God; and we know no way of becoming members of the Kingdom of God, save by baptism. Besides, the comparative silence of Scripture (if Scripture can be truly said to be silent) in regard to this matter is very significant. We do not commonly *say* much about settled and indisputable facts. The relation of the children to the Church was so universally recognized as a fact, a fact not disputed, that there was little occasion to refer to it in the Gospels and Acts of the Apostles. Yet there is just the mention of it, and the implication of its existence that we should expect to find, — the Shepherd's tender care of the little ones of His fold, His taking them in His arms, His declaring them "blessed," His provision for their nurture in His parting injunctions to His disciple, "Feed My lambs." In addition to this weighty testimony of Holy Scripture, we have the universal custom of the Church, not seriously disputed for centuries, — a fact of deep significance to every one who understands that he receives the Holy Scriptures themselves upon the same testimony.

Think of a flock of sheep without any lambs in it. It would be absolutely ludicrous, were it not at the same time so painful. The gospel did little for the Jews, if it took the men and the women into the Church, and left the children out; and that, too, when the Lord of the Kingdom says that "of such is the Kingdom." Really, to one acquainted with all the grounds of, and reasons for, infant baptism, as appearing from the Scripture alone, it is difficult to understand how a thinking and learned man can be a Baptist. Yet there are such men who are conscientious Baptists. Then, when you add to this the whole force of catholic consent through ages, it becomes a wonder greater still.

But, the main difficulty in the mind of a Baptist

is in the thought that "children can receive no benefit from baptism." This difficulty arises, altogether, out of a misconception of the nature of baptism. The Baptist regards the sacrament as involving too exclusively what *man* has to do in the matter. We, on the contrary, regard it chiefly as something that God does for man. It is not simply a profession of one's faith, but a reception into the Kingdom, into the family of Heaven. Our birth of the flesh is our entrance into creation: it puts us among God's creatures, in the great kingdom of Nature. Whereas, our baptism is our introduction into God's family, therefore properly and significantly styled the "*Kingdom of the Father,*" which involves the idea of our regeneration, our new birth, our second birth, our adoption and incorporation into the mystical body of the dear Lord. Now, we all admit that children can become citizens of another kingdom than that in which they were born. They can be made partakers of all the privileges of citizenship, in so far as minors can exercise them, or they can be exercised in their behalf. They can receive the benefit of all properties given, and they can have the protection of the law, and the right of having guardianship, etc.; in a word, they can have all the substantial benefits of citizenship, whilst yet they are all unconscious. What man would reject an inheritance for his child because the child could not understand the value of the gift? Furthermore, when they shall have reached years of discretion, they can say whether they will confirm and ratify the deed of their parents, and confirm the citizenship given them by their parents, or choose another for themselves, and thus give a deep significance to their confirmation. All this the Baptist ignores, — honestly, I doubt not, but still actually. He took up his Bible, and went to work to make out a scheme of church polity for himself anew, never sufficiently considering that a Church already existed, — a Church that had brought to him the very Scriptures which he was using as if a new revelation, not only separating himself from its government and guidance, but from its communion, and the church-members from communion with himself. He thus created a schism in the body, and established a sect in its very idea schismatical. If the Baptist idea of the Church be well founded, then for centuries Christ had no Church on earth; and then, of course, the Church had failed; and yet, of that Kingdom, there was to be no end.

Such are the conclusions necessarily and actually involved in the position of the Baptist. He does not sufficiently consider (and in this he is not alone) that the Church antedates the written word of the New Testament; that those Scriptures were written to meet the wants of an existing Church. The Epistles were addressed to the various churches. The Gospels are histories of our Lord's deeds and words, and were written after the events which they record; and therefore it is, that we have to go to the Catholic Church to find out what is the Word of God. These are very simple facts, but unknown to, and unweighed by, great numbers of men, who, in some other respects, are quite intelligent, and well informed.

The ultimate fate of the Baptist, as it regards the preservation of "the faith," it would be hard to predict. His want of a fixed Creed and Liturgy deprives him of a great security against error. His congregational character bereaves him of a great deal of good and restraint and guidance that come from mutual helpfulness. His extravagant reliance upon individual interpretations of Scripture opens the way to an unlimited number of sects, between whom there exists only the one tie, — of immersion in water, and infants rejected. The name of the Baptist sects is becoming Legion. The "*Campbellites*" (or "*Disciples*" they claim to be called) is one of their most prominent off-shoots, as yet but little known in the world at large, but numerous and aggressive wherever they have made a lodgement. Individualism bursts into full bloom under their favoring auspices. Every man can be a preacher, and every woman if she claims the privilege. With no established creed, and unlicensed power to interpret Scripture, there must be as many actual creeds as there are divergent opinions, with no protection, that appears, from the most fatal heresy. The atmosphere around them in some localities will keep them orthodox longer than their system would warrant. My children, adhere steadfastly to a communion which holds a fixed faith, and breathes it in every note of prayer and praise.

Perhaps I ought to say a word about what the Baptists claim for "*immersion.*" I feel that I am touching what is a matter of small moment in itself; but yet I must recognize it as having importance, because so much is made of it, to the prejudice of many tender consciences and weak minds. To a Churchman, it can hardly become a practical question, for *his* first concern would be to know if the minister proposing to baptize him had any commission thereto. The Baptists are always arguing the point of "*how to baptize;*" leaving out of view the question, "Who is empowered to baptize?" Yet the matter of immersion troubles some people, and huge volumes of immense research have been evoked by the water controversy. To me it appears like the question, "How much wax is to be put upon your seal in order to give validity to its impress?" It tends, moreover, to withdraw the mind from the sacramental idea to the material one. It is a small matter, it would seem, whether the water goes over the subject, or the subject goes under the water. It makes one sick to think how men can wrangle over such questions. They surely have never divined the true idea of a Sacrament, which is "the outward and visible sign of an inward and spiritual thing." One may as well contend that one must eat a full meal in order to receive the Lord's Supper, as to argue that you must be drenched in order to be baptized.

Without entering at large into the question, which would take me quite beyond my limits, I content myself with saying that the *quantity* of water is quite an immaterial part of the Sacrament (the Church manifests her characteristic wisdom and benignity in allowing both modes); that the practice of affusion seems to have been, as I fully believe it was, the primitive mode; that there are accounts in Scripture of baptisms where immersion was scarcely possible; that affusion can be practised everywhere, among all nations, in all climes and localities; that immersion in some climes and localities and seasons is impracticable, and that, therefore, it is more reasonable to suppose that where an ordinance was to be of universal obligation, the mode of its administration would properly be one of universal practicability; it being in accord with the analogy of God's dealings, to accommodate the Divine requirements to human necessities; that baptism being made (equally with the Sabbath) "for man," the mode thereof would likewise be adapted with the same wise and benignant accommodation to all men, in all climes, and under all circumstances.

Looking at the whole matter from this larger view-point, the insisting upon a special mode of receiving men into Christ's Kingdom, — which is never exactly decorous, as in the case of woman; sometimes harsh, as amid the rigors of winter; sometimes impracticable, as in countries where little water is to be found, — is not a reasonable thing, and is not in harmony with the genius of the Gospel of our Lord. Strange it is that some good, and reputed great, men take quite the opposite view. They see nothing in the Scripture accounts but immersion, immersion: whether in the crowded streets of Jerusalem, where thousands were unexpectedly baptized, or in the jail at Philippi at midnight, they always imagine full fountains, and overflowing streams. Even in the people's flocking to Enon, near to Salim, "where much water was," the practicability of immersing is the first moving cause to these brethren, who seem to look at all these accounts with a water-lens. They never stop to ask, how little water would suffice to baptize many men? — a good-sized baptistery would suffice — and how much water would be required to quench the thirst of a thousand camels upon which the people went to "Enon"? — ten camels requiring more for their satisfaction, than a thousand men for baptism by immersion.

The Baptist theory of essential immersion, stands out in the whole scheme of Redemption, not grand indeed to my vision, but solitary and peculiar, often harsh, and in some instances impracticable. Happily, it has made itself exclusive. The worst thing about it is, that it oftentimes becomes the "fetich" to the ignorant white and black man. It satisfies his senses to the full. He is all over a Christian when dipped. In a great number of cases, it ends the whole matter. His teachers do not believe or tell him any such thing, I am well assured; but the extravagant stress which they put upon the "dipping," — a process which separates him from all other Christians, and all other Christians from him, — naturally produces the result in weak and ignorant people.

THE METHODISTS.

The Methodists constitute a very large and influential body in the United States, and exist as a denomination in Great Britain and her dependencies, and have missions in foreign lands. Their government is Episcopal, made so by the assumption of the Episcopal functions on the part of two of their presbyters, who had been sent out to the American Colonies by John Wesley, the founder of the sect. Much controversy has arisen as to the intentions of John Wesley. There is evidence enough to show that he did not intend to form a sect in England, apart from the Church of England, where there was a national Church established; and yet, there is also evidence to show that he did contemplate the organization of a distinct sect in the American Colonies, although he disapproved of the assumption of the Episcopate by Coke and Asbury, his superintendents in the Colonies, and held it up — as it deserved to be — to ridicule: "Call me a knave, dear Franky [Dr. Francis Asbury], but not a Bishop." Wesley had the sense and churchmanship to know that he, a Presbyter, could not make a Bishop. But Wesley's intentions, whatever they may be claimed to be, or proved to be, are of no moment; for the question is one of *authority*, not of Wesley's *intention*.

The founders of Methodism were men of zeal, earnestness, and power. They preached with unction some of the great truths of the gospel, and encouraged the emotional element to a great and enthusiastic degree. The low condition of piety in the Church of England at the time greatly favored the growth of the sect. Had the English Church acted with the wisdom and forecast which have marked her more recent administration, Methodism might have been utilized and controlled. The Church of England greatly needed a stimulus. But unwise counsels prevailed; and the Methodists, especially in the United States, took a determinate movement away from the Apostolic Church. Wesley himself never left the ministry of the Church.

His followers very early took ground against domestic slavery; and the pressure of this question had divided the body into "Methodists North," and "Methodists South," before the breaking out of the civil war. So great was the mutual repulsion on the part of the two bodies thus divided, that they have never yet been able to come together in legislative union, notwithstanding the fact that slavery — the original cause of the division — no longer exists. Unhappily, the Methodists have become in the Northern States too much of a political power, and candidates for the Presidency find it to their interest to play into their hands. As they have gained in political power, they seem to have declined in piety and religious zeal (I refer now to the Methodist Church North), and are gradually losing some of their strictest notions of certain matters pertaining to dress, amusements, and the like, — the ultimate fate of all Puritanism. Their organization is one of great power; and through their varied functionaries, they manage to move the whole body of the Communion by the will of a few leaders. Two of their Conferences thanked Congress for impeaching President Andrew Johnson before his trial took place. In some particulars, they are more like the Church of England and her daughter in America, than any of the Denominations. They still retain a considerable portion of the Book of Common Prayer, in a mutilated form, and they use it at funerals, marriages, baptisms, and celebrations of the Lord's Supper; thus showing, that, when they wish to draw especially near unto God, they resort to the use of a form. But yet, at the same time, it is the fashion of some of their preachers to declaim vehemently against the use of forms in worship. Such is man's inconsistency. They cannot be said to have any "distinctive denominational principles," — as do the Baptists, — but owe their growth and extension to their zeal and diligence, which I have ever admired in them, and am glad to recognize at all times. Their founders — Wesley, Whitefield, etc. — were men of power; and they were all brought up in the Church of England, and taught by Church mothers in the Church catechism, baptized, confirmed, and ordained by the ministry of the Church of England. Some years ago, a party rose up among them who protested against having Bishops, and claimed that laymen should have a voice in their legislative bodies. It is surprising, that, with the last-named popular claim to public favor, the Protestant Methodists — for such was their name — should not have had a larger following; but they have never become a large body; and now that the Episcopal Methodists have admitted to some extent lay representation, they appear to have lost much of their original prestige, and will probably die out.

CONCLUSION OF MATTERS PERTAINING TO RELIGIOUS ORGANIZATIONS.

A WORD more just here in regard to the Protestant Episcopal Church, — the Church of my forefathers, so far as any records go. My descendants will find, as I have found, that the Church of their forefathers presents to them all that man needs to enable him to live a religious life, and at the same time to maintain that individuality and freedom of thought without which religion can have no charm and no enduring power. She gives us the ministry in unbroken line from Apostolic days, and the Catholic Creeds, and none other, as the doctrinal conditions of communion. She gives us for our rule of life, the commandments of God and the precepts of Christ. She leaves it to "societies" to add to the faith and the law. She provides a mode of worship, simple, majestic, and reverential, where all men's needs are provided for, and the great and good God is worshipped "in the beauty of holiness." In her legislative action, there is guaranteed, as far as human sagacity can guarantee any thing, safety and protection for all who come within the reach of her authority. The constitution and canons of the Protestant Episcopal Church in the United States are, in my judgment, and that of wiser men than I am, the justest and most conservative body of laws and canons that have ever been framed by men. Every order and estate of men in the Church is cared for. Class legislation is impossible under her system. Her whole history has been marked by so much wisdom, moderation, and conservatism, that wise, moderate, and conservative men have been drawn to her by elective affinity. What a record is the roll of her children! Her teachings are specially adapted to enlighten the ignorant, to raise up the lowly, and keep down the proud. Hence, the multitude love to go where they can be exalted. I desire no higher honor than to have my name registered in her roll. I ask no greater security for my children than that they may be found in her ranks. I have no higher ambition than to be found at the last day among her true followers. For my brethren and companions' sake, I wish her prosperity. Above my chief joy, I prefer her — Jerusalem, my mother!

Let me say a word just here. There are some few in our communion, who manifest an undisguised aversion to the Protestant character of our Church. The desire to drop the name of "Protestant" is with some, I fear, the indication of this aversion. If I thought that this was the underlying *animus* of all who favored the change, I should retain the name at all hazards; because the conflict then would be for principle, and the name would be the flag around which every true son of the Church should rally.

There are some in our midst who decry the Reformation, and disparage the great reformers. I have only one word for them. As I view the matter, they are not honest to their vow, "to preach the gospel" "as Christ hath commanded and this Church hath received the same." We have a pure and majestic ritual: let us not ape any other system. Some scientists think that men ascended from the monkey. I have not witnessed that phenomenon, but every now and then I am satisfied that I have seen a man descend to the monkey. I heard the Bishop of Sodor and Man make a speech at Wolverhampton, England, some twenty years ago. He concluded by saying, "Finally, my Brethren, beware of monks and monkeys." For my part, I had rather see a man a monk than a monkey; and I occasionally suggest to some youthful specimens of the latter species, "If you don't like the 'Reformed Church,' the 'unreformed' Church has its doors open to receive you. Go home! In the name of truth, sincerity, and decency, so far as in you lies, be what you purport to be. Use the language of the Bible and of your mother, the Church, and speak not in dubious and long since discarded phraseology of 'masses,'" etc. Sometimes, when I hear of a certain kind of priests bewailing the Reformation, and using such phrases as "wretched Latimer," etc., the doubt will rise in my mind whether such men would not prefer to have piled additional fagots about the stake, rather than to have gone up with those glorious martyrs in chariots of fire to Paradise.

SCEPTICISM, RATIONALISM, AND SCIENTISM.

I HAVE thrown these three together for convenient handling, and not at all to ignore or confound the distinctions between them. Just now they seem to be playing into each other's hands ; and, by their "flocking together," they seem to be in some sort "birds of a feather." The rampant spirit of rationalism in common life, in the public press, and, sad to say, in the pulpit and at the altar, allies itself with a vaunting scientism, and together they have engendered a spirit of scepticism, which threatens the very existence of faith itself. Where do you find the spirit of a Newton and Bacon, accepting alike, with a childlike mind, — the only safe mind, — the teachings of Revelation and the conclusions of a stern inductive philosophy? Bacon truly and grandly said that the entrance into the Kingdom of God and into the realms of science demanded the selfsame spirit, — that of the child.

I wish, above all else, for my children, that they shall believe in Christ. If there is no reality in Christ, then our life goes out in darkness : — I leave my children without the sun, and I take my leap in the dark. But you will perhaps say, "What must I believe? there is so much diversity of opinion : what is truth?" I answer, Christ is "The

Truth;" "Christianity"—a term not known to Revelation—is but vague and uncertain; "Christ" is one and the same, "yesterday, to-day, and forever:"—of this more anon.

If you take a superficial view of the distracted condition of Christendom, you will be tempted at times to think that there must be some serious cause for uncertainty where there is so much diversity of opinion. Not so: a deeper view will bring you to a sounder conclusion. Let me illustrate my meaning. Suppose, by way of illustration, that a dozen men are called to the witness-stand, to testify in a given case. They all differ in their testimony upon certain points of evidence; but upon certain other points, vital and fundamental, as all confess, they all agree. What conclusion would you come to? Naturally and reasonably, I think, to this conclusion; viz., that the matters upon which they are all agreed are fully proven, and not less fully proven because of their diversity of statement of certain other particulars; indeed, more satisfactorily proven because of that diversity,—the diversity going to show that there is no collusion among the witnesses.

Now, apply this illustration. Nearly all Christian people, of whatever name, are agreed upon the matters of faith set forth in the Creeds of the Church. (The exceptions are so small as to be inappreciable in a large and comprehensive view of Christendom.) Now, these Creeds contain the vital facts of the Christian faith, — the Fatherhood of God, the Incarnation and Atonement of Christ, and the Personality of the Holy Spirit, the Life-Giver, Sanctifier, and Comforter. The truths set forth in these Creeds are so vital and all-pervading, that a belief in them entitles such believer (so far as his faith is concerned) to baptism and membership in Christ. The Christian peoples affirming this faith are divided among themselves in many points, — points of religious opinion, ritual, polity, and usages, — but they are *one in "the faith."* Christendom thus, indeed, presents from this point of view an undivided front. The main line of the Church Militant is unbroken, notwithstanding a few divisions have been routed and scattered or captured. What, then, becomes of the arguments used by infidels and scoffers, that they know not what to believe in view of the divided condition of Christianity? If they will accept only the faith in which Christendom is united, and accept it as rational beings should accept such a faith, they will be good Christians.

Moreover, as it regards morals, all Christians are united in accepting the law of God, interpreted by Christ, as the rule of a Christian man's life. Let any man live up to those precepts of Christ, which all Christendom accepts, and he will live a godly and Christian life. How strong, then, and hitherto unassailable, is the line held by the Church Militant, — "the blessed company of all faithful people." I might pause here to note how weak, lamentable, foolish, and wicked a thing it is for any Christian man to do any thing to weaken the strength of this line by needless and ambitious divisions, but this is aside from my present purpose.

Infidelity, in every age of the world, has planted itself for the overthrow of Christianity — as yet, without any serious break of the line of Christian truth. Every argument that the wit of man and the malice of the Adversary could devise has been levelled against it, so far without success. Every new discovery in science has been peered into to find a weapon with which to attack the intrenchments. The heavens have been scaled, the ocean sounded, the bowels of the earth have been ransacked, with this same hostile intent. Jews, Turks, infidels, heretics, and scientists have made common cause against that system which will yield to none, and would fain save all. Yet the faith still survives and triumphs. A wonderful and sublime spectacle it is indeed, inspiring and strengthening the faith of all who declare that of "this Kingdom there shall be no end." Modern scientism, with the same intent, has gone to work, with a diligence, eloquence, and research worthy of a better cause, to batter down the walls hitherto impregnable. Its highest achievements, were it to accomplish its purpose, would be to deprive man of God's Fatherhood, quench the light of revealed truth, destroy all hope of immortality, and range the race of men among the brute creation, — an animal only of a higher order.

It is a matter of profound interest to inquire whence this spirit was evoked which would bring such a blight upon the fair creation. If it were the necessary conclusion of science, which it is not, one would think it would be reached at least with a sigh or a moan. But there are men who can render the whole world Fatherless without a sigh; extinguish every hope beyond the grave without a pang; and dissolve the faith of centuries without a tear, alas! I have no quarrel with science. Christianity has none. Her sphere never traverses the orbit in which science has its being. Science, truly so called, is the handmaid of revealed truth. It is the opposition of science, falsely so called, which we have to encounter. Where science stops, having reached its uttermost verge, and finds forces and powers which elude investigation, and baffle all inquiry, there revela-

tion begins, and discloses to faith the Divine
Fatherhood in the Great Creator, in Whom all
things live, move, and have their being. The
present favorite theory of what are called advanced
scientists, is that of evolution, not development,
which latter is always in manifest working. Under
this theory of evolution, not only the lower creation, but man himself, mind and all, is the product
of endless series of growth from an original germ
— they call it "Protoplasm." There would be no
serious objection to this theory, if it had any
adequate proof to sustain it; but so far, it is
announced and heralded without sufficient creden-
tials. No scientific theory can claim our acceptance until it has received what we may call
"catholic consent." The same rule, you will observe, holds in regard to scientific truth as to
revealed truth. The theory of evolution has not
received universal acceptance, even among scientific men. Astronomy *is a science*, — has its fixed
laws, and prevails by catholic consent. It is not
yet so with evolution: it is still under trial and
investigation. The scientist, as does the sectarian, flies off from the catholic system, and attaches
himself to a "school" of thought. Like the sect-
ist, he parades his individuality, and founds a sect
in philosophy. Meanwhile, you can afford to wait
for the conclusions of science. Receive them as

true, and adjust yourselves to their logical requirements. If the theory were true, they have only removed the difficulty a step farther back. They have not quit themselves of the necessity of an original creator. For whether the Creator, by virtue of His omnipotent power, created all things after the *genera* in which they now exist, or created the original material, out of which all things were successively evolved, there is equally a necessity for an original *creative act.* Therefore, evolution, if it were true as a theory, and proved to be true by induction, could not affect the truth of the being of a God, — the first truth in natural as in revealed religion. Therefore, in so far forth as the existence of a God is concerned, they, the theorists, may safely go on with their theories; but they will ever find, and find it pretty soon, a force, a life, or whatever they may choose to call it, permeating all things, explaining all things,— itself inexplicable. They call it "the *'unknowable.'*" They have reached the end of their line: it has run itself out, but they have not touched bottom. Yet they vaunt themselves upon having found the unknowable. One would think they would be touched with something of humility and reverence, but I have failed to see that spirit; rather that of vanity — strange that man's vanity should be inflated by the discovery of his ignorance! Practically, however, the theories of the modern scientist have tended, in a great many minds, to obliterate the sense of a God, and to diminish faith in all Divine revelation. This is its practical outcome among great numbers, showing, I think, how easily people will become credulous when they have no faith: having not the truth, they will clutch at its caricature. I have read much of the writings of these men. They seem to be what we would call *smart* men: they do not strike me as *profound* men. They do not impress me as Plato and Aristotle and Shakspeare and Bacon impress me. They seem, in comparison, to theorize and chatter. I have great sympathy with a modern writer who is reported to have said, "I am content to find my ancestors in the Garden of Eden. Let those who prefer otherwise, seek theirs in the 'Zoological Gardens.'" But one thing they do; and for that, all good and true men must hold them accountable, if at no other bar, at the bar of decorum and reason. Their influence goes to destroy alike the sense of God, and to lower the dignity and responsibility of man. The revealed Word — which I cannot throw away for the sake of an unproven theory — the revealed Word, I say, proclaims that at creation, God made man, and made him as He made nothing else; did not evolve him by gradual processes from lowest germs, but made him after His own image, and endowed him after His own likeness. I cannot throw away that truth, with all that it involves of human dignity and possible immortality, for an undemonstrated theory. Surely, what St. Paul said of the heathen of his day, is true of the heathen now in the midst of Christianity: "they did not like to retain God in their knowledge." O my children! Come not ye into their assembly; unite not your honor to such as these! These men are not blessing their race by any moral earnestness. They are not founding your homes for the destitute, the widow, and the fatherless. They are prating;—"ever learning, and never able to come to a knowledge of the truth." Learn the principles of science (as Newton and Bacon taught them), and you will never be beguiled by the fallacies of scientism.

Evolutionists of the most advanced school tell us that man, starting from the simplest forms of matter,—mind itself being but "a mode of brain-motion,"—and evolving by gradual processes, is moving on to perfection; that thus, finally, all evils will be rectified, all disorders adjusted, all rights recognized, and the regeneration of society fully accomplished. The antagonisms and discontent of the laboring classes, the struggles of woman for what she claims as her rightful co-ordination in human affairs, etc.,—all these are triumphantly pointed to as indications of the progress of society to its perfect consummation. In all such prognostications, the influence of the Christian religion is by some disparaged, by some ignored, and by others utterly repudiated as a superstition, barring the way to a more rapid progress. These men glory in the fact that they have nothing to do with any thing save "*phenomena;*" and by that expression, they mean the phenomena of the material world, counting nothing *real* save that which is *material*.

Yet there are phenomena in the world of mind which cannot rationally be ignored, and which must be considered, classified, and explained. There are questions which force themselves upon the mind, and which must be answered in some way. They demand an answer. Such a question is this, for example, "What think ye of Christ? whose Son is He?" It will not do to say that this question is irrelevant to the scientific mind. He stands face to face with this undeniable and pregnant fact, that, only in those parts of the earth where the Christian religion prevails, is there any marked advancement, even in science and in the industries and arts of life; and that the only heathen nations which are now manifesting signs of awakening life—as China and Japan—are those which have felt the quickening influences of contact with Christian peoples. This question, and other questions of similar import, cannot be contemptuously thrust aside, and relegated to the "domain of metaphysical investigation." They are matters of fact — as much so as any in the domain of physics; and are quite as worthy of observation as the anatomy and habits of bugs and reptiles. The indifference of some so-called wise men to the study of "final causes" is to me an astounding phenomenon, and causes one often to doubt whether every man is indeed a truly rational being. I met with a disciple of this school some time ago. Such men abound nowadays; — smart indeed, but not very profound; dealing with the surface of questions, and contemptuously ignoring all consideration of the final causes of things visible or invisible. We fell into discourse upon religious matters. I urged upon him the importance of considering such matters: he replied that he "had no faith whatever in Christianity; that he had read volume upon volume on Christian evidences, but they had made no impression on his mind;" and concluded by saying "that it was not worth while for us to argue the matter, because there was no common ground from which we could start." I then asked him "if he did not think it the duty of every man to try to bring himself, by culture and labor, to his highest possible perfection?"— "Unquestionably," he replied. "Well, then," said I, "here is a ground we can both start from. Now, in the effort to bring your character to its highest perfection, must you not have some rule, standard, or model by which to work? The artist who wishes to make a representation of some object in nature, say a tree, or horse, seeks out the best specimen of such object, and aims to reproduce it, does he not?"—"Yes," he said, "assuredly."—"Then," I urged, "in trying to bring yourself up to your highest capability, would you not, for like reason, cast about you for the best specimen of human character, in order that you might have the advantage of a model to work by? You would not reasonably look within yourself for the ideal man. The effort to make yourself a better man implies, that, as yet, you know yourself to be an imperfect one: in making yourself the ideal, you would be only repeating and reproducing yourself, would you not?"— "No," said he, "I would not look to myself. I would take some better specimen than myself for a model: I would properly take the best man that I knew, and try to imitate his virtues."— "Now," I urged, "who is the best man that ever lived?"—"I know of but one man without sin," he very reverently said. "Who was that man?"—"Jesus Christ."—"Then, does it not follow from what you have admitted, that, in the effort to perfect your character, you should set before you for imitation Jesus Christ?"—"I see no way of evading the conclusion," he admitted; "but I did not anticipate reaching such a conclusion." There is no way by which the above conclusion can be evaded, save by denying the supreme excellence of Christ; and to this depth the dreariest infidelity has rarely fallen. Surely, the man of science, the sociologist, the philanthropist, can join in with the devout believer, in his most exalted mood, and all with one acclaim crown Him the Christ, Chief of all, "*the One among ten thousand, the One altogether lovely.*"

In this connection, let me further press the point, viz., that the scientists, *even from their stand-point*, are bound to meet the great question of questions, "What think ye of Christ? whose Son is He?" For if it be true, as they affirm, that man has been evolved from lowest forms of matter, and is to ascend, by continued evolution, to his highest perfection, how did it happen that the most perfect specimen of manhood appeared at the beginning of the Christian era?—assuredly not the most advanced era in history. According to the accepted system of the philosophers of this school, Christ should have appeared at the culminating point in evolution, and not at the inauguration of His era. How came He to antedate the final consummation? He has certainly done so. Every advancement in morals and social order at the present day is but an approximation — as yet, faint indeed — to the style of human life which He set forth in His teachings, and exemplified in person. All the beneficence of this, the most beneficent age of the world, in its care for the diseased, the destitute, and the outcast, finds its spirit and impersonation in Him Who "went about doing good." He is the luminous point in all history. His influence is the greatest known. His birth constituted a new era in time. All that man in the times before Him knew of the rights and humanities of life was in Christ renewed, enlarged, illuminated; with much added that they knew not of. All that man has truly taught since, and is now truly teaching, of the relative duties of life, can be found in His precepts, and exemplified in His sublime life. The observance by all men of the Christian rule of life would bring about confessedly a millennial age. Prophets converge in Him. Apostles radiate from Him. At this hour, the better part of the world, as it moves on and forward, looks back to Him for guidance, as oarsmen, propelling the boat, ever look back, as they row, to their helmsman. When human nature shall have reached its possible perfection, it will be because it has been more and more imbued with the spirit of Christ. Wars between capital and labor, jealousies of caste, social antagonisms, and all wrongs, will cease when men shall be like Christ, when the laws of trade shall be superseded by the law of love, and every man shall "love his neighbor as himself." "Love worketh no ill; therefore love is the fulfilling of the law." Now let the men of science answer the question concerning Christ, "Whose Son is He?" They cannot answer it from their standpoint. Their doctrine of heredity furnishes no clew to *His* parentage. From what they know, they must let that question rest in still silence.

But take the Christian view, — that, not by natural generation, but by a supernatural incarnation — the Word of God becoming flesh — He, the Son of God — that is His heredity — came among men, — then all these questions, which cannot otherwise be explained, are fully answered. St. Philip said to the Master, "Lord, show us the Father, and it sufficeth." Yes, it sufficeth, — it covers the whole area of human need. The cry of Philip is the cry of suffering humanity, "Show us the Father." The answer which came from Christ responsive to this cry, is the crowning knowledge to poor, struggling, and weary men. "Have I been so long time with you, and yet hast thou not known Me, Philip?" "He that hath seen *Me*, hath seen the *Father*." Would you, my children, become acquainted with God, your Father, and be at peace? then study Him, not only in the realm of nature, where He so gloriously manifests His power and wisdom, but seek to know Him as mirrored in His only begotten Son, our Lord Jesus Christ — the "Brightness of the Father's glory — the express Image of His Person."

Let nothing shake your faith in this foundation, which is elect and precious, — which has stayed the hopes of millions in past ages, and affords the only refuge and footing for the generations to come.

"Let no man deceive you with vain words." Let no pretensions to profoundness in the smart men of the age for a moment beguile you. I have ever found profound men to be men of faith. They see deep enough to know that behind and below all physical phenomena, there is a great, first, and intelligent Cause, in whom all things live, move, and have their being. "He that formed the eye, shall not He see?" Such men, instead of staggering at the mysteries of Revelation, accept them, in childlike faith, as the crowning proof of the exceeding love and graciousness of the Father, Who did not create a world in which He could not send His Word to His children — ay, more, send Him to take upon Himself their nature, to talk with them, and tell them of duty and danger, how to live and how to die, and thus how at last to find their way home to the Father's house, that they might dwell with Him forever. What a contemptible and dreary conception of the great and good Creator must they have, who cannot reckon it possible that He can guide and bless His children, hear their prayers when they cry unto Him! A wise man would not make a machine which he could not guide and control according to his will. But I must close this long letter to you, my dear children. You will read these lines when I shall have passed away from your companionship, and shall have solved for myself the mystery of life and death. I end with an extract from my last will and testament, written before these lines were written. Speaking of my children and grandchildren, I write, —

"I leave them my love and benediction. I ask of our Father for them no earthly honors or emoluments. He will give them 'food and raiment,' and 'godliness with contentment,' if they 'seek first His kingdom and His righteousness;' but I do, with all my heart and soul, desire that they may have a good and well-grounded interest in the Divine love and favor covenanted to them in Christ Jesus, our most blessed Lord and Saviour. I exhort them to reverence, and to cling to the traditions of their house, and to be ever loyal to that branch of the Church of Christ in which they received their baptism and nurture. I feel assured, that, though absent from them in the body, I shall be ever near them to the latest generations. I love them, and desire their welfare beyond all power of expression. 'Fear God, and keep His commandments; for this is the whole duty of man.'

"Avoid debt, my children, for debt brings with it a multitude of ills. 'Owe no man any thing, but to love;' and this debt of love, which we must owe to our fellow-men, is a most precious obligation, and the constant recognition of it in deeds of kindness gives a flavor to the whole life.

"It is not necessary to live luxuriously, nor even to live comfortably; but there is a deep necessity that you should live honestly.

"The Lord of life gives us the true philosophy of life. 'A man's life consisteth not in the abundance of things which he possesseth.' One of His chief Apostles, who had learned from the Master this lesson of life, has left behind him this record of himself — and what a record it is of the battle of life well fought and gloriously won! — 'I have learned, in whatsoever state I am, therewith to be content.'

"I would rather be assured of your having gained this height of self-abnegation and faith, than to know that you would outrank in wealth the millionnaires of this generation. Worldly wealth is of time, and passes away with time. 'Godliness, with contentment, is great gain:' it is treasure laid up in heaven, beyond the reach of time, chance, or change.

"You will hear ofttimes that this or that passion is the root of all evil. The divine Word, with which a large view of life always tallies, declares that 'the love of money is the root of all [forms or descriptions of] evil.' It is pre-eminently the root of present existing evil. Now, whilst I am writing these lines, our people are in a craze. The spirit of speculation has made some wise men mad. Some will become rich; many more poor; the great mass of both rich and poor demoralized. This speculative spirit not only runs counter to the Christian code, it is in the long-run disastrous in a prudential point of view. The difference between legitimate, wholesome business and speculative trade is essentially this: in the one, all are profited, — the producer, the intermediary, and the consumer; in the other, the success of one is at the loss of his neighbor. This state of things is not only irreligious, but unwholesome. It is of the essence of gambling. Under its baleful influence, I see men all around me going down with a run, — 'erring from the faith,' 'falling into snares,' and 'piercing themselves through with many sorrows.'

"'Thou, O man of God, flee these things, and follow after righteousness. So shalt thou find peace at the last!' One approving look of the dear Lord, one gracious word of His, is of more value than all the honors and riches of the universe. As I stand at this moment on the border, and look back and forward, these truths, taught me in childhood, and impressed upon me by all my observation and experience of life, assume great distinctness. That only will survive all change and decay which links one in with eternity, and is as imperishable as the soul, — even the 'faith in Christ which worketh by love, which purifieth the heart, which giveth peace with God through Jesus Christ our Lord.'

"My father gave his life to the sacred ministry. Of course, he left no money to his children. He left, however, an unsullied name, and the record of a useful and honorable life, — a priceless heritage indeed. He left for the guidance of his children, among a thousand-fold suggestions, three special admonitions. I have tried to heed them, and I transmit them now for your guidance: —

"'Owe no man any thing, but to love.'

"'Be indifferent to the judgment of man: seek only to do what is right, and let your life speak for itself.'

"'Be careful not to make issues: but, having made them, maintain them at all hazard to the end.'

"Now unto the gracious mercy and protection of the good and great Creator, the God and Father of our Lord Jesus Christ, I commend you, my children, now and evermore. Amen."

POST-BELLUM REMINISCENCES.

It has occurred to me that the incidents recorded below might afford my children some valuable information and entertainment. They throw some light on this part of our country's history, and, I think, should see the light.

INTRUSION OF THE MILITARY POWER.

Just after the civil war, which reduced the State of Alabama to the condition of a military province, your grandfather became the object of a military order which closed the churches of his diocese, and subjected him to a notoriety which he neither desired nor anticipated. It is a long story, with which I will not burden these pages. You will find in the journals of my diocese a very full statement of the whole matter. You will also find a brief synoptical view in the "Centennial History of the Church in America." Let it suffice for me to say, that even at this hour, as I stand upon the border of time, there is not a word put down in the history of those events which I regret or would recall. I have in this matter the answer of a good conscience towards God and man.

I give you here the briefest outline. When

the war ended, I found the civil government of the State subverted, her constitution abrogated, her governor deposed, and held under duress, her whole civil power annihilated, the drumhead the only tribunal of justice.

The first practical question that pressed upon me for decision was that relating to the use of the "Prayer for all those in Civil Authority," as formulated in the Book of Common Prayer. I looked around, and found no vestige of any such authority. I was under no ecclesiastical obligation to use the prayer as it stood in the prayer-book; for when I was consecrated a bishop, I had made a "Declaration of Conformity" to the Constitution of the Church in the Confederate States.

Some of the generals of the Federal army were kind enough to step forward, and attempt to solve all my doubts upon the question; but they did not succeed in settling my difficulty. Prayer ought to be a very real and sincere thing; and I could not find it in my heart to send up a prayer to Heaven for a blessing on what had no existence, nor could I make up my mind to pray under dictation. But I was bound by a higher obligation than any which man can impose, to pray for our rulers of whatever sort. The fact that they were holding us in slavish subjection did not release us from that obligation. Nor did we desire any such release. The fact that they had abrogated all the sanctions of our former legislative, judicial, and executive government, only increased the necessity for more earnest prayers unto God that He would give grace to these soldiers who held us under the bayonet, to "execute justice, and maintain truth." But when it came to ask the Almighty to give "health, prosperity, and long life" to the commander-in-chief of this body of men, who had settled down upon our whole country, and when officers with swords at their sides came to demand it, I, for one, had no doubt or misgiving as to what course I should pursue. I wish that some of my brethren who will not consent to catholicize our prayers — the prayer for the President is the one uncatholic spot in our regular liturgy — could have seen the necessity as I then saw it. The wording of this prayer will have to be changed. The troubles in this country have not ended. We will have to go through all the diseases incident to a nation's childhood. We will have — we have already nearly had — rival Presidents-elect. It may be we shall have a President of Knights of Labor, with men of brawn and muscle to make good their pretensions. Then will come the strain; then timid people will palter with the Almighty in a double sense; then feeble brethren, at the nod of a soldier, will wing heavenward their extorted little prayers (which are insults to Heaven), with protests attached to them. I have known that to be done, and it may happen again.

He studies history to little purpose who does not now provide for all the contingencies likely to arise in the course of events. What endless troubles came upon the people of England during the usurpation of Cromwell. The loyal men of the realm felt bound in conscience to pray for the king; and the powers that were forbade it, and sent the offenders to prison or into exile. A state of things may exist in this country, when a rude soldier shall step up to the officiating minister, and demand to know which President of the United States he refers to in his prayer; and it may even happen that one clergyman may be praying in one church for one President, and another in a neighboring church may be invoking long life and prosperity upon another claimant to the office. He has read history very superficially who does not recognize the possibility of all that I have supposed.

Situated as I was after the war of the States, with no existing civil authority over me, I was virtually ordered to "pray for the dead" with but slight hope of any present resurrection. They who mean nothing by their prayers can easily pray for any thing or nothing. "Why do you curse so?" said an acquaintance: "you offend me by your profanity." — "Ah, well!" was the reply, "you pray a good deal, and I curse a good deal, but the Lord knows that neither of us means any thing by it."

But this is aside. In the state of things above described, I issued a pastoral letter to my clergy, and told them that "the prayer for all those in civil authority" was out of place and utterly incongruous under the present state of affairs; that, whilst bound ever to pray for our rulers, there was a manifest incongruity in the prayer-book form of prayer for rulers which made it inapplicable to our people in their then condition; that it was not a question of loyalty, but of congruity, and a question to be settled by none but an ecclesiastical authority. The clergy fell into line to a man.

Hearing that there were troubles brewing in Mobile, — I had refugeed in Greensborough, — I went there at once. I had been in the city but a few hours, when a servant came to my room, and told me that an officer had called to see me. Upon going to the parlor, a general of the Federal army introduced himself to me as an officer on the staff of the General commanding, and said that he had called by direction of said officer, to know when I meant to use the prayer for the

President of the United States. I told him that that was a question the General had no right to ask, and that I answered no such questions if put in a tone of authority; that the Church had her sphere of action, and could not permit any intrusion. The officer was thrown aback, talked a good deal about the absoluteness of military power, and intimated, not obscurely, that I would have to succumb. I told him that he would see for himself the issue. After a considerable talk on his part, — I preserving entire silence, — he proposed that we should talk the matter over as "between man and man." I told him that I had no sentiment that was not open to the world, but none that could be extorted.

He then in a very familiar way put the question anew under the programme of, as "between man and man." — "When do you think you will use the prayer-book prayer for the President?"

I answered, "When you all get away from here." This particular prayer was for a government of the people's choice and affection, — the loyal prayer of the Church of England, rather servilely continued in our liturgy. "The fact is, sir, that the government, as it is over us now, and impersonated in the President, is a government for which I desire the least 'length of life' and the 'least prosperity' that is consistent with the permissive will of God;" that we did ardently pray that he who held these reins of absolute power might have "grace" to execute judgment, and to maintain truth, etc., and hoped that our prayers would be answered. I then said to the officer, "Suppose our positions reversed; suppose we had conquered you, and, amid all your desolation and sadness and humiliation, commanded you to fall down upon your knees, and ask God to grant long life, health, and prosperity to our commanding officer, — would you do it?" I cannot quote his reply, for his excitement threw him off his balance; and he intimated in strong but profane terms, that he would be — something very dreadful — if he would. "Well," I said, "I am not disposed to use your phraseology; but, if I do that thing that you come to order me to do, — addressing the Almighty with my lips, when my heart is not in my prayer, — I run great danger of meeting the doom that you have hypothetically invoked upon your own head." He then left.

In the course of a few days, there came out "general orders," shutting up all our churches, and "suspending" me from all my functions. These orders were, on the part of the general commanding the military district, accompanied with a shower of bad language that could only fall with its foul savor on the head of him who gave vent to it.

Meanwhile, the churches were nearly all closed, and soldiers stationed at the doors to prevent entrance. Yet it is a great mercy that even military rule cannot entirely close our communications with Heaven. We worshipped in private houses; and I confirmed in churches which were not guarded by soldiers, issued Pastorals, etc., much to the indignation of the general who had suspended me from my functions.

After a while, the Council of the Church in the Confederate States held its regular triennial session at Augusta, Ga. There the whole question of "the prayer for those in authority" was settled by the adoption of the old form in the Prayer-Book. Coupled with this action, however, was a "resolution" that each bishop should exercise his own discretion as to the time for its introduction. Upon this modification, I had absolutely insisted.

By this action of the Council, it was competent for me at once to order the use of the prayer; but as the military intrusion still existed, I delayed the matter until the order should be withdrawn. It went hard with the General to do it; but he was compelled by a higher power, and poured out his wrath in language that could only defile the lips from which it issued.

If I cannot say with the Apostle, "I have, after the manner of men, fought with beasts at Ephesus," I can truly say that there was poured upon my head a very flood of abuse and obloquy. I received it in all complacency. I do not know whether I most enjoy the plaudits of my friends or the abuse of my unfriends. It is grateful "*laudari a laudato viro.*" The abuse of some men is a crown of glory.

Now, I have made a long story very short. The whole narration might prove wearisome.

RE-UNION OF THE CHURCHES NORTH AND SOUTH.

I HAVE dwelt at length upon this matter in the Memorial Sermon of Bishop Elliott, and it needs to say but little more. As I have before said, my own position was quite anomalous, because of my having been consecrated during the civil war. As a matter of course, the matter of Church re-union was among Church people the all-absorbing theme. The Southern Bishops looked at the matter from different stand-points, and came to different conclusions. Some of them took the ground, that, as the necessity for the formation of a Church South had ceased, the Council thereof should dissolve of itself, and the Bishops and dioceses, through their representatives, should appear in General Convention at Philadelphia, as if no separation had taken place.

Others took a different view, and thought it best and most expedient to keep up the Southern organization until the *animus* of the General Convention should have been made manifest. Without going into the matter any farther, and without questioning for a moment the sincerity and conscientiousness of any one, it will suffice to say that the *legislative* re-union — for there had been no breach of unity — took place without serious difficulty, and that all was settled harmoniously, to the great comfort of all who love and "pray for the peace of Jerusalem."

I feel bound, however, to suggest one thought in this connection. Bishops Atkinson and Lay, two of our most able and revered Bishops, did appear and take their places in the "General Convention," which met in Philadelphia, in October, 1865, and did not appear at the meeting of the "General Council" of the Southern Church, which met in Augusta, Ga., in November following. Their course in this respect was entirely consistent with their view of the situation, and it must be said to their honor that they did not take their seats in the House of Bishops in Philadelphia until they were entirely satisfied that every interest with which they suffered themselves put in charge had been fully protected. In making my recognition as Bishop of Alabama, a condition precedent to their action, they deserved my thanks, because their intention was kind; but I feel it incumbent upon me to say that their interposition was never sought or expected by me. I knew that my position was peculiar, from the fact that I had been consecrated during the war, and no consent asked from the ecclesiastical authorities North. I had, therefore, fully determined to resign my jurisdiction, if my case constituted a bar to re-union.

Much credit attaches to the course pursued by Bishops Atkinson and Lay in proceeding at once to Philadelphia, and it is generally said that their presence there tended more than any thing else to the promotion of re-union. Doubtless, their action had such influence; and I would not write a word in disparagement of the course pursued by them. I must say, however, that there was another influence brought to bear upon the spirit of re-union, — the absence of such men as Bishops Elliott and Davis. It meant a great deal. There is no divine sanction in the legislative union of dioceses; and their absence meant, "Let us wait, and see what it will be best for us to do."

Dear brethren, all of them. They have passed

into a higher realm, and how infinitely small must appear to them now the little perturbations of their mortal state!

There was one infelicity only attending the whole matter. The House of Bishops, in consenting to my exercising jurisdiction in Alabama, coupled with their action an expression of "fraternal regrets" on account of my Pastoral in relation to the use of the prayer for the President of the United States. I did not like it, but I passed it by. I made many allowances for that action. It was to some a hard matter to swallow, and the opportunity of flinging a passing regret seemed to make it less unpalatable. In relation to this particular point, I merely observed — in my history of the whole affair, which is contained in my address to the Diocese of Alabama — as follows: "It would seem, that, in restoring old relations, the expression of 'regrets' is in order; and it may not be amiss in me to state, that, after careful review of the various pastorals put forth in the last unhappy years, there are very few in which we, who look at all that has taken place from a different stand-point, have not found occasion for 'regrets,' to which we can give no adequate expression."

It is inexpressibly sweet and refreshing to one who for truth's sake and a good conscience has been misrepresented abroad, to come home and stand among his own people, and hear from their lips the "well done" of a universal approbation.

I summed up to my diocese a history of my whole course, and closed in these words: —

"Thus happily, as I think, the Church in Alabama has been able, through God's grace and kind Providence, to do her full duty, and to maintain her dignity and propriety, and, looking alone to the weal of the whole body of Christ, to pursue a steady and consistent course. Henceforward, guided by the same spirit which has thus far led us and governed all our deliberations, let us more than ever strive for those things which concern the glory of God and the good of His Church.

"The indications are, that there is a glorious future for this branch of Christ's Universal Church. We are able to show to the world that we are not a sect, much less a sectional sect; that the catholic spirit of the Southern dioceses has met a like response in the catholic spirit of the Northern dioceses, — deep calling unto deep, — giving us confidence that henceforth, as ever before, no political differences shall prevail to break the bonds of catholic unity and heaven-born charity."

The whole address, with all its details, was referred by the Council to a committee, which made the following report in the form of resolutions that were adopted without dissent: —

"*Resolved*, 1st, That the firm, dignified, and Christian manner in which the independence and dignity of the Church in this Diocese have been maintained by its Bishop, the Right Rev. Richard H. Wilmer, D.D., during the trying ordeal of the last year, has elicited our admiration, and deserves our cordial thanks.

"*Resolved*, 2d, That the explanation and defence of his course, as set forth in the address to this Council, place his conduct on ground that must challenge the assent and approbation of all just and thoughtful men.

"*Resolved*, 3d, That the Bishop be requested to furnish a copy of his address, for publication.

"These resolutions, on motion, were considered *seriatim*, and unanimously adopted." (Journal of Council for 1866.)

In connection with the foregoing reminiscences, and forming a part of the whole subject, I give you below a copy of a letter which I wrote Bishop Hopkins of Vermont immediately after the close of the war of the States.

The good Bishop — and the Church in the United States has furnished no finer specimen of a learned, brave, and independent Bishop — addressed a circular to the Southern dioceses, urging them to return without delay, and as a matter of course, to their old relations with the Church in the United States. Our wounds were still bleeding, and a little time was needed to heal them over. But the letter will best explain itself.

A REPLY TO BISHOP HOPKINS' CIRCULAR LETTER TO THE SOUTHERN BISHOPS, BY ONE OF THEIR NUMBER.

Mobile, Ala., Aug. 1, 1865.

Right Rev. and dear Sir, — I have just received a printed circular, addressed by you, as senior Bishop, to the Bishops of the Southern dioceses.

The tone of the circular is such as we might have expected from one who is never unmindful of the rights and feelings of his brethren.

There is one point, however, in reference to which you will pardon me for saying a few words; and I need not assure you that I do so with the utmost deference.

In your pamphlet addressed to the Southern Church, in the year 1861, and in your recent circular letter, you take the ground that the existence of a separate legislative organization in the Southern States "would be clearly schismatical." In your letter you say, "and no theologian denies that a wilful and needless separation from the Church would be clearly schismatical."

True, no theologian denies this proposition; but there are many who will deny that the maintenance of a separate *legislative* organization amounts, of itself, to a "*separation from the Church.*" The minor in the syllogism is here assumed, and constitutes the very point in debate.

Is the Church in the United States "*separated*" from the Church in England? Yet they maintain distinct legislative organizations. Can any two branches of the Church of Christ be properly said to be in a schismatical position — the one to the other — whilst they have a common doctrine and discipline, and maintain an unbroken recognition and intercommunion? Schism, as defined by the standard authorities, has reference primarily to the rending of communion, and cannot be truly predicated of branches of the Church of Christ which maintain intercommunion.

No well-ordered mind can doubt that it is, for obvious reasons, highly expedient and desirable to have one ecclesiastical organization in one Nationality.

Nay, more, it would seem to be desirable, if

practicable, to have only one such body, with powers so extensive, in Christendom.

But there is a condition of things which may render it still more *desirable*, and indeed *essential*, to have national organizations; and circumstances may arise which will render it expedient to have distinct organizations within the boundaries of the same civil government — as, for example, in the case of the Episcopal Churches in England and Scotland.

You say, in the sentence already quoted, a "*wilful and needless separation*," etc. You therein seem to take the ground, that a failure on the part of the Southern dioceses to come into legislative union with the General Convention would amount to a "*wilful* and *needless* separation," etc. Permit me to say that the separation was not originally wilful, nor, in our judgment, needless. Whether a continued separation be wilful and needless will depend upon circumstances not yet foreseen. It is, therefore, if you will pardon me for so saying, premature to pass judgment upon that point at the present time.

We of the South have not, at this moment, sufficient data upon which to found a deliberate and well-advised action. We do not know what concessions and admissions may be required at our hands. We have no concessions or admissions to make; and, therefore, there are some of the Bishops and their dioceses which will maintain the organization of the "General Council," in order to be prepared for all contingencies whatsoever.

Were all men, good Bishop, like-minded with yourself, we might have no hesitation in this matter; but certain painful things are brought to our ears.

One party proposes "to keep the Southern Churchmen for a while in the cold;" "to put the rebels upon stools of repentance," etc. We see in the Journal of 1862, certain resolutions proposed, pronouncing certain worthy Bishops "schismatical," and proclaiming the jurisdiction of another Bishop "null and void." True, the resolutions were not adopted, but they indicate the temper of a part of that body; and we have no means of ascertaining the complexion of the next "General Convention." Fanaticism grows fast in the hour of triumph.

Again, a well-accredited rumor reaches us that the Pastoral prepared by yourself did not suit the temper of the House of Bishops, and that it was supplanted by one which gave the Church utterance in matters political.

Now, suppose that the ensuing General Convention should decree that every deputy from a

Southern diocese should, as a preliminary to taking his seat, be required to purge himself,—to admit that the secession of the Southern States was a "rebellion," and that the organization of the General Council was a "schism,"—in what a position would the deputies from the South be placed? This is not an impossible, nor an improbable, supposition in view of the present pressure of the reigning fanaticism. The Presbyterians and the Methodists appear disposed to take this attitude towards their membership in the South. We have indications, on all hands, that the Church has absorbed the sectarian element much more rapidly than she has assimilated it to her spirit. There is another feature of this subject not to be overlooked, and one which you cannot perhaps, to the full, appreciate.

It is commonly remarked that the restoration of the union between the Churches, North and South, is a *"mere question of time,"* and that, therefore, it is best to do at once what must, sooner or later, be accomplished. But there is something due to sentiment in this matter, and the healing influences of time must be permitted to have play. In questions which involve sentiment, *"the time"* is an important element, and the logic which excludes it will greatly mislead. In some matters, *the time of action* is every thing.

There is nothing illegal in a second marriage, and it is generally a "*mere question of time*" with men when they shall marry again; but, "The funeral baked meats do coldly furnish forth the marriage tables."

The best men of the South are now under the ban. I cannot now recall the name of a single man, of those who have been ordinarily selected to represent the Southern dioceses in General Convention, who is not, in the estimation of public opinion at the North, "a rebel and traitor." But, more than this, they are classed under the President's proclamation as "unpardoned rebels and traitors." And this for obvious reasons. The prominent men of the South in the army attained a grade which now excludes them from the general amnesty; the highest legal talent was placed in judicial positions, the occupancy of which renders them liable to the extremest penalties of the law; the best talent in commercial and agricultural life has been so unfortunate as to accumulate property above twenty thousand dollars in amount.

Now, from these classes of men, — men who have achieved position, — the Church would naturally select her deputies to the General Convention. It is a most significant fact (and one which must be understood, in all its bearings, by the Northern mind, before deputies from all sections of the country can meet together in becoming harmony, and needful mutual respect), that the men whom, from our stand-point, we regard as the most truly loyal, and in all respects trustworthy, are precisely those who are stigmatized by the people of your section, and by your Bishops in their Pastorals, as "rebels and traitors." It is surely not unreasonable to assume that your people are honest in their opinions, and that they will be consistent in their actions. Treason is surely a dreadful crime. It may, therefore, reasonably be expected that they who denounced their Southern brethren as "traitors," will question the propriety of allowing them to take part in the deliberations of a "loyal Church." For aught we know, there may be a majority of the next General Convention who will be disposed to take this ground; and I, for one, shall respect their consistency, whilst I cannot but lament their bigotry.

Moreover, the Southern deputies themselves may very naturally be supposed to have some sentiment in this matter. Their sons and brothers lie in bloody graves; their lands are desolate, and strangers devour it in their presence; their emancipated slaves garrison their cities; they live themselves, as yet, under the ban; their representative man, no guiltier than themselves, is in bonds, and may have to die an ignominious death. The whole Southern people, therefore, are at this moment awaiting trial in the person of their representative head : they are denounced as felons, and a shackled press is forbidden to speak a word of vindication or remonstrance. Your own heart, good Bishop, will tell you that men in such a condition are in no mood to join in *jubilates* over a restoration which is sealed by their degradation. The peace, for which Te Deums will be chanted, is purchased by the loss of their inheritance, and they are now sitting in the deep valley of humiliation. The men of the South have no desire to prolong the hopeless conflict. They accept the failure of their effort as a fact, and, as Christian men, will render a faithful allegiance to "the powers that be," for God's sake ; but it is asking too much of them that they shall swell the pageant which celebrates their subjugation. Some time, Bishop, must be given to the heart to school itself. Our people are in no mood for joyous congratulations. They are not yet out of mourning for their dead. It is easy for you to come together, and to join heartily in *laudates* for peace and reunion. Yours is the victorious section. It is easy for him who triumphs, to forgive ; and from your stand-point, you can thank God with a full heart. We are trying to forgive and to forget;

and, lifting up our hearts unto God from the dust, we are trying to say, "Thy will be done." You do not know, dear Bishop, what we have to endure; and your people "love to have it so." You will doubtless say, that the Church of God is "not of this world," and that, as Churchmen, we should take no note of these things. But, alas! the whole Journal, Pastoral, etc., of the Church North, savor of these things. The next General Convention will beyond peradventure, discuss these things. The delegations from the various dioceses are even now marshalling for the conflict. Loyalty is now at a high premium, and the various religious bodies of the country will vie with each other in the struggle for popular favor. The Union sentiment just now is uppermost in the public mind, and there are those who will train the legislation of the Church to catch the propitious breeze. That religious body will come just now into most favor, which renders itself most demonstratively loyal. We shall have, before long, tracts and books dedicated to the popular idol; and the strongest "Reason why I am a Churchman" will be, not only that the Church is truly "Republican,"— that has long since been sufficiently proven,—but that she is thoroughly "loyal."

Excuse some of us, Bishop, for preferring just now to stand aloof from the discussion of these subjects. Our own wounds are too recent to bear rough handling. We have no heart for them. We have no wish to discuss them, for there can be no free discussion. Nor can we, by our silent presence, be faithless to the memory of our dead, nor consent to stand by whilst others inscribe "traitor" on their gravestones. It is urged that we should act together and at once, lest the Roman Church should, by her united front, win the prestige of the hour. We all comprehend the reason of Rome's indifference to this American conflict. She is not native born. Let the recent agitations of Italy, let her history for twelve centuries, testify as to whether the Church of Rome does always stand so serenely aloof from the political excitements of the day. Rome is not the mother of this child. She cares not whether it be divided or not. The judgment of a Solomon, therefore, is not required in disclosing the secret of her present indifference.

We have a great work before us in this country, —to maintain Church supremacy within her sphere, and to thrust politics out of doors. In order to this, we shall be compelled to catholicize our prayers. The Church has suffered, and is now suffering, incalculably, from one local and political prayer. Scenes of violence have desecrated her sanctuaries, the clergy have been driven from their flocks, and the sheep scattered. Sadder than all, the Priests of God have succumbed before His altars at the beck of military dictators.

Should the *animus* of the next General Convention be such as to commend itself to the heart and mind of the South, there will, I think, after a while, be no general disposition to keep up a separate organization. The General Council will be held, according to adjournment, at Mobile in November next. Its action, as a matter of course, must be somewhat affected by the *animus* exhibited in the General Convention. This *animus* we cannot, from the nature of the case, very clearly foresee; and we are not in a position to exercise any control over it. We shall act, as the Church in the South has hitherto acted, dispassionately, and in view of the best interests of the Church. We cannot, however, be frightened from our propriety, nor can we be deterred from the adoption of any measures that may seem to us best and most expedient by the cry of "Schism!"

Whilst having all the elements of a perfect branch of the Church of Christ, — the Word, the Ministry, and the Sacraments, — and being, in so far as our will can effect it, in perfect unity — both organic and subjective — with the Catholic Church, we can still pray from a full heart, "From all schism, good Lord, deliver us," and think not, no, not for a moment, that we violate catholic unity, although we may not be represented in the General Convention of the Church in the United States.

I sent you some time since a copy of the Pastoral which I issued to the Diocese of Alabama at the close of the war. This Pastoral related to matters upon which we in the South have not altogether agreed among ourselves. I could not come satisfactorily to any other conclusion than that presented in the Pastoral. There should be reality in prayer, if nowhere else. The duty of the Church is, unquestionably, to pray for all in authority, of what kind soever. This she does in her litany and elsewhere. But the *particular prayer* in the liturgy, as its history proves, was conceived and worded with a special and very marked reference to the subject of the prayer,— "Civil Authority." In her Articles the Church declares the duty of obedience on the part of her members to "civil authority, legitimately and regularly constituted." It is this description of authority that the Church prays for in the prayer headed, "For all in civil authority." For this she cordially entreats a long continuance and prosperity. At this time measures are in progress which look to the restoration of "legitimate and regularly constituted civil authority" in the

State of Alabama. When such authority is restored, the clergy of Alabama are required to resume the use of the "prayer for the President of the United States and all in civil authority."

The above is substantially the letter which I wrote privately to you upon the receipt of your printed circular. I think it due to myself that this letter should go forth to the Bishops of the Church, in order to define my position, and to show that, in declining your invitation to be present at the General Convention, I am not acting without, at least, some show of reason.

Depend upon it, dear Bishop, that any restoration of our ancient relations, which looks to the establishment of lasting harmony in the Church, must be based upon a good mutual understanding, and upon a due regard for the rights and feelings of all concerned.

And now, dear Bishop, allow me to say that I have for many years regarded with veneration your faithful, consistent, and impartial maintenance of the truth, and to express the hope that you may long be spared to bless the Church of God by your counsels and by your example.

Yours faithfully in Christ and in the Ministry of His Church,

     RICHARD H. WILMER,
      Bishop of the Diocese of Alabama.

Rt. Rev. J. H. HOPKINS, D.D., *Bishop of the Diocese of Vermont.*

NOTE BY BISHOP GREEN.

BISHOP WILMER has read to me the above letter; and I so fully concur in its sentiments, that I adopt it as my answer to your circular letter, addressed to the Bishops of the Church in the South.

WM. M. GREEN,

Bishop of the Diocese of Mississippi.

REV. WILLIAM H. WILMER, D.D.,

President of the University of William and Mary.   Departed this Life 1827.

HAVING finished my personal reminiscences, I give you a sketch of my father. I was too young to be able to speak of him from my personal knowledge.

I scarcely know how to express my gratitude to the Rev. Philip Slaughter, D.D., of the Diocese of Virginia, for putting it in my power to hand down to you the following sketch of your great-grandfather.

Dr. Slaughter still lives, and bears fruit in his old age. He is the historiographer of the Church in Virginia. Although now of extreme age, he still revives the past, and, as our "Old Mortality," keeps from oblivion the memory of noble deeds and noble men.

REV. WILLIAM H. WILMER, D. D.

The following is a sketch of Dr. Wilmer in Mr. Slaughter's speech at the late jubilee of the Theological Seminary. The subject is comparatively new, and is exhibited from new points of view with new illustrations. The Episcopal Church in Virginia is so much indebted to this clergyman, that we are sure Dr. Slaughter's brief history of him will be read with deep interest, and, we trust, with profit. Some of our younger readers may need to be told that Dr. Wilmer was the father of Bishop Wilmer of Alabama, and of Rev. Dr. George Wilmer of Williamsburg, — at this writing, Professor of Divinity at Sewanee, — and the uncle of Bishop Wilmer of Louisiana, and that he was also one of three brothers, all of whom were clergymen of the Church.

William H. Wilmer was born 1782, in Kent County, Md. In his boyhood he received deep religious impressions from a pious aunt, which were confirmed during a severe illness, when, he says, he felt himself to be lying in the arms of a loving Father, Who looked upon him with a reconciled countenance, and he felt the "peace that passeth all understanding."

He was educated at Washington College, Kent County, Md.; and his religious principles and demeanor became subjects of mockery to the boys, who reproached him with a want of manliness in not joining them in swearing and gambling. He was overcome by the pressure for a time, and joined the boys in their wicked sports. But his conscience became so clamorous that he could not silence its voice, and he concluded it was better to endure the mockery of the boys than "to be in hell amid everlasting burnings."

He resolutely refused to go again to a mill which was the scene of their sports. So they turned him over, as they said, to the Methodists, as serious people were called in those days.

But (as he told one of his parishioners afterwards) he did not care what they called him, since the best man that ever lived deserved no better monument than this, "*A sinner saved by grace.*" He told a daughter of Professor Campbell that he was about seventeen years old when "he took hold of the covenant for himself." "I felt that the precious gift of faith was given to me, that I was justified freely for Jesus' sake, and, being born again, the love of God was shed abroad in my soul by the Holy Ghost given to me." "As soon," he continued, "as I felt that I was accepted by God as His son, the thought flashed upon me, What church shall I join? My heart responded, The dear old neglected Episcopal

Church; and under her banner will I fight the good fight against the world, the flesh, and the Devil."

He was ordained by Bishop Claggett in 1808, and for several years had charge of his native parish of Chestertown, Md. In 1812 he came to Virginia (Dr. Henshaw says, "at the instance of Mr. Meade"), and as rector of St. Paul's Church, Alexandria. The most cursory inspection of our journals of convention will show the prominent part which he played in the drama of the restoration of the Church and the foundation of the seminary. He was chosen by ballot to preside over the convention of 1814, and preached the convention sermon, — a sermon which for felicity of style, soundness of doctrine, force of argument, and power of appeal, is unmatched in the Virginia Church-literature of that day. In this sermon he says, —

"When the sons of Judah escaped from the house of their prison, and returned again to build the temple, the foundation could only be laid by removing the splendid ruins of the desolated sanctuary: then came the remembrance of its former glories to mind, and they wept aloud.

"Have we not equal cause for sorrow in the view which the desolated sanctuaries of the Most High in this State present? As we hope, then, to repair the desolations of many generations, as we hope to preserve the virtue and happiness of our nation, as we hope to transmit to posterity the valuable inheritance of a form of sound words, as we hope to obtain that honorable and valuable eulogium, 'Well done, good and faithful servant,' let us seize the present moment to strengthen the things that remain, that they die not. This morbid insensibility which has crept upon the Church is, perhaps, not the sleep of death. It may be the crisis of her disease. We will yet hope that the system retains sufficient *stamina* for its resuscitation. Her doctrines and liturgy are yet unimpaired: and she furnishes in the principles and early prepossessions of the present generation a just foundation of hope, that, if her energies were directed by a proper administration, she would yet 'arise from the dust, and put on her beautiful garments;' that she would yet come forth from her exile 'clear as the moon, bright as the sun, and terrible as an army with banners.'

"Let us arise, and redeem our honor, and that of our venerable Church. The eyes of Virginia are fixed upon us. To us the thousands who perish for lack of knowledge stretch forth their hands. From us they demand their portion of that inheritance under the New Testament, of which we are the trustees and administrators. To us the Church looks for the confirmation of her best hopes. Leaders of the armies of the living God, to us is offered this first of honors, to us it is given to fight, if in the post of trial, also in the post of honor; to us it is given to be covered with stars and laurels and honorable wounds, and to have a memorial more grateful than to be embalmed with a nation's tears."

After this sermon the ballotings proceeded; and Bishop Moore was elected Bishop of Virginia, —the old man eloquent, whose heart was a deep well of sanctified emotion, overflowing in tears from his eyes, falling in musical cadences from his lips, and streaming like electric sparks from his gray hairs, and from his trembling hands, and producing a sensation the like of which had not been seen in our Church since the era of Devereux Jarratt, the morning star of the Virginia Reformation, whose mantle Bishop Moore so touchingly invoked the first time he entered Old Sapony. Dr. Wilmer was always President of the Standing Committee, and often of that on the State of the Church, and the author of many of their reports. He was always at the head of the delegation to the General Convention, and presided with distinguished ability over the House of Clerical and Lay Deputies for four successive sessions. He was an active member of the Committee on Canons and of the Prayer-Book Society, and indeed of other committees, of whose reports he was generally the draughtsman. He, with Mr. Oliver Norris, according to Bishop Meade, imported the Canon on Clerical Discipline from the Maryland code. In 1818 he recommended that the clergy be requested to take students for the ministry into their families, and that they might be licensed as lay-readers. The Education Society, which was the true mother of the Seminary, — whoever may have been its father, — was a realization of these views, and was organized the same year, he being its President so long as he remained in Alexandria. The "Repertory" contains stirring addresses from this Society, of which he was the author. In 1819 he, with Mr. Hawley and others, established the "Theological Repertory," which was the organ of the society, and the loud champion of the Seminary in every emergency, and from whose pages a discerning critic might extract a volume of theological literature of no small merit from his pen. In 1820 he recommended the project of Dr. Smith for a Theological Professorship in Williamsburg, and in 1821 he advocated its establishment and the appointment of trustees, all of which was done. He made the first report from the trustees of the Seminary; peculiar circumstances, he said, making it necessary to cherish such an institution in the South. In 1822, the Convention of Maryland having resolved to establish a Theological Seminary in that diocese, Dr. Wilmer was elected President of the Faculty. Bishop Kemp laid his hand upon this scheme, and crushed it; and thus by an act of Providence, the friends and funds of that institution were transferred to our Seminary in its time of need, adding material and moral support to our infant institution. In 1823, Bishop Moore having been detained by business from the Convention, Dr. Wilmer was elected its President.

Professors being wanting in the Seminary at Alexandria to aid Dr. Keith, Dr. Wilmer generously consented to take charge of the departments of Systematic Divinity, Ecclesiastical History, and Church Polity, without fee or reward, in addition to his heavy duties as rector of St. Paul's Church, Alexandria, which had been built in 1818 to accommodate the large congregation which had overflowed the old church.

In 1824 he called upon the families in Virginia who had spare books, to send them to Dr. Keith, as the nucleus of a library for the Seminary. He was also the author of several addresses in behalf of the "Episcopal fund;" and, in response to Judge Washington, President of the Colonization Society, he prepared a paper in which he condensed the merits of that institution within a small compass.

Dr. Clemson, of the class of 1825, in a letter to me, giving pleasant memory of his Professor, says, " Dr. Wilmer was a bland, cheerful, companionable man : the students found him very affectionate and accessible — his manner inviting confidence. He was a very popular pastor. He and Mr. Norris had services in the evenings of the week which were of a social character, and in which the students were invited to exercise their gifts. All the Professors were men who honored their calling as Ministers and teachers. I revere their memory, and revert with sad pleasure to those happy days. The opening years of the Seminary were very auspicious. They were wise and true men who made a choice of such fit instruments for laying the foundation on which has been reared so grand a superstructure to the glory of God. Dr. Wilmer received and declined an invitation to be the first rector of St. John's, in Washington, and another to be assistant to Bishop Moore in the Monumental Church, in Richmond, because his friends thought his presence necessary to the Seminary. But in 1826 he thought he heard a call from heaven to the Presidency of William and Mary College, with the care of Benton parish, Williamsburg ; and he obeyed the call. His career in Williamsburg, according to Rev. Mr. Charles Mann and other contemporaries, was attended with a perfect ovation. In the language of some of the old citizens, he took possession of the town. He visited from house to house, without regard to denominational distinctions: and one old resident, still living, says, that, during his first winter there, the people seemed to forget their customary dancing-parties; and prayer-meetings, and social singing of psalms and hymns, took the place of popular amusements. His colloquial powers and his wonderful tact were illustrated in many social scenes. At a wedding, the musicians were about to be summoned to inaugurate the dance; but the host would not allow them to enter until the Doctor's consent was had, and a young lady was commissioned to sound him. He replied, "This is not my house; but, as I am commanded not to conform to this world, I can retire to the hinder part of the ship, and go to sleep." — "But, Doctor," she said, "when you were a child, did you not love to dance?" He replied, "Yes; but when I became a man, I put away childish things. You, Miss, are no longer a child; and it is high time that you should put away childish things, and live for more important ends." The conversation continued; and, one by one, the company came within the charmed circle, fascinated by his felicity of speech, until the dance was forgotten, and the entertainment ended with a word of exhortation, singing hymns, and prayer. The remark was heard on all sides, " What a delightful evening we have had!" When Dr. Wilmer first went to Williamsburg, many of the students were indignant. One of them was heard apostrophizing the college-walls, and saying, "Old William and Mary, thy glory is departed: a long farewell to all thy greatness, since a Priest has come to be thy governor." This young man being very rude to the Doctor, the latter inquired of my informant the reason of such conduct. She explained; and the doctor replied, "I will overcome his evil with good;" and with such address did he manage the case, that the young man was soon heard to say, "What a fine man he is! so fearless in doing his duty, and yet so kind!" I could multiply these illustrations, but time and space forbid. I may group them in some other form, and give them to the public. Bishop Meade says, in his article on "Benton Parish," "Never before had the experiment of reviving religion, and of converting young men, been so earnestly employed." Prayer-meetings were held twice a week in private houses, and the first-fruits of a genuine revival of religion in college and town had appeared.

But Providence had other designs. Being about to leave Williamsburg on a journey, and being anxious to have all the children baptized, he rode around the parish in a heavy rain, begging those whose children were unbaptized to bring them to the Saviour for a blessing, offering, where no fit sponsor could be had, to act as such himself. His exposure brought on a chill, which ended in death on the 23d of July, 1827. He said while he was conscious, "I know that I shall die. The Lord's will be done."

The last thing he said was, when hearing the voices of his family praying, and being told on inquiry what it was, he said fervently, his countenance lighting up for a moment, "It is right, very right;" and fell asleep in Jesus. On the occasion of his death, the people rose up, as one man, to do honor to his memory. He was buried beneath the floor of the church; and members of the various denominations united in placing a tablet on the wall, and defraying the funeral expenses.

Bishop Meade, on behalf of the trustees of the Seminary, said, —

"We have to record the heavy loss sustained by the Board in the death of the lamented Wilmer. In this, and every other department of usefulness, he ever displayed a judgment, zeal, and activity seldom united in one man. The emblems of mourning, which now designate the members of this convention, evince the high esteem in which his services were held by the whole Church."

Bishop Moore said, —

"It is impossible for me to find language to express my sense of loss by the death of our beloved Wilmer. He was one of those who first called my attention to this diocese. Of these, but one survives; and he, I trust, will be spared to assist you with his counsels when my head shall be slumbering in the dust. He was a man of business and piety. As a preacher, he was faithful, energetic, and eloquent. He was the friend of evangelical religion, and considered that the strictest regard to the order of the Church was perfectly compatible with the most animated social worship in the houses of his parishioners. His private meetings, in his opinion, were the nursery of his Church. Like St. Paul, he not only taught his people publicly, but went from house to house, exhorting them to prepare to meet their God. His fidelity met my earnest approbation; and, if it is the wish of the clergy to give an account of their stewardship with joy, oh, let me entreat them to go and do likewise!"

Such is an outline of the life of this gifted man of God. It is not a full-faced and full-length likeness. I have the ideal and the material, but not the time, nor perhaps the skill, to realize it in a lifelike picture, — adjusting the lights, and making the mind breathe from the face, and the "eloquent blood mount into the cheek, and almost speak." Dr. Wilmer had an uncommon combination of physical, intellectual, and moral energy, which was the secret of the incredible amount of work he did in the parish, in the press, in the pulpit, in letters, and in untiring visiting the sick and the poor and the afflicted, fatherless children and widows, and pursuing the sinner through all the mazes of his madness, until he was caught, clothed, and in his right mind. There are fruitful fields of illustration, at which I have only glanced in passing. Among these are his missionary excursions through Virginia with Bishops Moore and Meade and Allen and McGuire and others, in which he was eminently successful in rekindling loyalty to the Church, in erecting many a family altar, and in warming many a heart that had grown cold. He left his mark all along the wayside, — the passing traveller, the laborers in the fields, and, indeed, all classes, from the old, powdered and ruffled aristocracy to the servant who held his horse, who received from him a smile, a word of counsel, and a blessing. Finally, if ever a monument is reared to the restorers of the Church in Virginia and the founders of the Theological Seminary, the truth of history demands that William H. Wilmer should have a high niche in it.

NOTE. — I am under obligations to Rev. George A. Smith and others for some of the interesting illustrations of Dr. Wilmer's life. Mr. Smith was a loving pupil of Dr. Wilmer, and is one of the few living depositories of valuable Church traditions.

REMINISCENCES OF RIGHT REV. J. P. B. WILMER, D.D., L.L.D., LATE BISHOP OF LOUISIANA.

I CANNOT refrain from placing in close connection with my own reminiscences some few words which will serve to convey to my children an idea of a good and great Bishop of the Church, who bore our family name, and gave lustre to it, not only in the United States, but in the Anglican Church throughout the world. He took a conspicuous part in the Lambeth Conferences of 1867 and 1878.

He deserves to be handed down to posterity in a volume rather than in these few pages; and I should have undertaken the grateful task long ago, if I had thought myself able to do this glorious man the justice due to him. I cannot even

attempt to give his likeness in miniature, he was so unlike all other men I have known, — so strong, and yet so gentle; so grand, and yet so approachable; so majestic in thought and diction, and yet so childlike in his familiar utterances. Bishops and peers would crowd to hear his mellifluous and golden words, and babes would reach out for shelter in his arms.

Men called him, rightly, the Chrysostom of the Church in America.

His father and mine were brothers, and both of them clergymen of the Church. His father, Rev. Simon Wilmer, was a grand old Roman. We grew up together as children, and loved each other with something more than a brother's love. My heart overflows even now when I think of him. I always want to see him. He seems about my bed, and about my path, and yet I cannot get speech of him. All his peculiarities, his absence of mind, his forgetfulness, instead of detracting from his influence, imparted a special charm to the whole man: we would not have had him changed, — "dear cousin Joseph!" as we all called him. I do not know any one whose life, if it could be drawn out in full, would so enrich our Church literature. The older he grew, the wiser he grew, the more profound in his generalizations, the more epigrammatic in speech, the stronger for truth, the sterner against error, the tenderer to the helpless and fallen.

In his best moods he talked as an inspired oracle, and with such wealth of language that the strength of his thoughts was almost buried in the beauty of his imagery, as a strong pillar of stone overgrown with flowers.

He always desired a sudden — he could never have experienced an unprepared — death. He wanted to spare others the anguish of the parting scene. He had his wish. In a moment, in the twinkling of an eye, he passed from the toil and perplexities and disappointments of life into the rest of paradise. I never have realized that he was dead. I never think of him as dead, but as being with the Prophets and Apostles, some of whom in many things he resembled, — Isaiah, St. John, St. Paul, and the like. He now holds high converse with those blessed ones, I doubt not. What grand themes, what lofty speech, what exalted hearts, as they cast their crowns down together, and adore the Lamb that was slain, and yet ever liveth to receive honor and adoration from His redeemed people!

I give you herewith an extract from the annual address which I delivered to the council of my diocese at its first session after his death: —

"The whole Church has been called upon to

lament the loss of my near and dearly beloved relative, the late Bishop of Louisiana. I cannot trust myself to speak at any length of this dear Bishop. The loss to me personally is irreparable. I feel as if I had lost part of myself. I know not that we had a divergent thought. For more than sixty years we had grown together in sympathy and affection.

"To those who knew him well, any description would fall far short of the living reality. To those who knew him not, a true portraiture would seem to be extravagant.

"There was in him that wonderful dualness of character which we find in all complete and fully developed natures, and which found its fullest and most perfect manifestation in Him 'Who was made man.' There was in him a wonderful blending of exquisite tenderness and sensibility with holy resentment of wrong; patient endurance of personal injury, coupled with burning indignation against injustice to others. This was the spirit that flamed in St. John, who, at one time, would fain have called down fire from heaven to consume those who treated his dear Lord with indignity, and at another would calm his fevered brow by resting it upon his Lord's bosom; the same spirit that made St. Paul at one time willing to be 'accursed for his people,' and, at another, forced him to hurl his 'Anathema,

Maranatha,' against any man who loved not the Lord Jesus Christ; the spirit which reached its absolute perfection in our dear Lord, 'Who for us men and for our salvation came down from heaven and became man;' Who, at one time, 'like a lamb, was dumb before His shearers,' and at another, like a lion, drove the profaners of His Father's house from the temple with a whip of cords. All large and well-rounded natures — '*teres atque rotundus*' — manifest this dualness of nature — the nature both of a man and woman — in a spirit which melts over the sufferings of a child, and yet can stand undaunted before rulers and Presidents, and to their face denounce their injustice and wrong. So near akin to holy jealousy is an ardent love.

"I would that some one could be found to give us a complete and faithful likeness of the dear Bishop of Louisiana. I cannot trust myself to attempt it. I make my own the eloquent words of one who knew him well, and loved him well, — one who had capacity to weigh magnitudes, himself a man of weight (Right Rev. Hugh Miller Thompson, D.D., then rector of Trinity Church, New Orleans, and now bishop of the Diocese of Mississippi). I had urged him to preach the bishop's memorial sermon. In reply, he writes, 'I am here by one drawing — the personal magnetism of a man whose soul was like a calm, deep, summer lake; whose presence stilled the warring of my own heart, its unrest and rebellion, and even doubt, I confess it; and in the light of whose transfigured face I found God's peace. He is gone, and that is gone out of my life which can never come again.

> 'Another beacon-light blown out above me;
> Another buoy-bell stilled upon the sea.'

. . . .

"The deeps, calm and profound, into which descended, and from which were reflected, all the starry lights of heaven, in that magnificent soul, were all I ever saw, and the memory of it all that remains unto me now. I don't know whether he was 'learned,' or 'able,' or 'eloquent,' or any thing else. I only know that his speech to me was like the chiming of the bells in the towers of heaven. I only know the personal presence of the man put me in harmony with the everlasting cadences. I want only to sit alone with a memory that ought to sanctify my life. The regal glory of that majestic face as I looked upon it for the last time in the coffin, can never fail from my remembrance. He looked, dead in his robes, a Prince of God; and the dead look was but a faint transcript of the living presence. I might clasp your hand, who knew him, kinsman, brother of the same blood, and say nothing but what the heart might say, but I could do no more.

"Our 'memorials' and our talks about him are idle enough, God knows, and, to some moods of mine, are even shocking. I cannot talk about him. The surface-babble about his absence of mind, and personal peculiarities and the rest, are infinitely disgusting to me. I ask for myself to be allowed to bear in my heart, as one of the treasures, and, God help me, one of the responsibilities, of my life, the fact that for three years I knew, associated with, and loved this man, crowned on earth one of the peerage and senate of heaven."

I add here some verses written to me by my sister, your aunt Marion. They were written at a time of deep depression in the State of Louisiana. A cloud of vultures had come down upon the battle-field, to prey upon the dead and nearly dying. Strangers held the reins of power, aliens sat in the halls of justice, and publicans gathered the tithes of cotton. I use plain language because I speak of a foul wrong done our people. Think of a set of people inimical to us, just out of a terrible war, leaguing with a dominating race of newly emancipated slaves, and exercising all functions, legislative, judicial, and executive — a humiliation such as in modern times was never inflicted by one civilized people upon another. At this time, the indignation of the people of Louisiana — for the pressure was then chiefly there — had reached such a pitch, that the noblest, bravest, and most loyal citizens had come to the solemn resolution that they might die, but would not longer live in this condition. I speak of what I know, and it strains the heart now to recall it. A single step farther, and the streets of New Orleans would have run blood. And yet this was the hour when it was proposed to me to hold a united "Te Deum service." The good friend who made the proposition suggested that we were all now under one flag, and a "Te Deum service" would be in good form. I replied that it was true that we were under one flag, but that the flag had a twofold aspect: it had its stars and its stripes; but the stars shone upon him, and the stripes alone were still upon us, and that just now we might sing "De Profundis," and even "Nunc Dimittis," but not "Te Deums," unless men could sing the same anthem under stars and stripes alike. I recall these things because I am writing reminiscences, and want my posterity to know the past, and how to interpret the deeds of their fathers.

This state of things which I am now describing will show how little the good people of the North — and for them I feel a warm admiration and regard — knew of the actual state of affairs in the South during this period. Their fathers groaned under a tax upon tea laid without privilege of representation. The sons of those men should comprehend the intolerable weight that the men of the South bore all those years. I asked a highly intelligent gentleman in New York how he would like his State Legislature to be composed of one-third of whites — many of them were not to the manor born — and two-thirds of newly emancipated slaves, and told him that such had been the constituency of the South Carolina Legislature. He said "it could not be possible." The fact is, that a full history has not yet appeared; but we must all appear at the bar of judgment in time and eternity.

At this crisis, the Bishop of Louisiana came forward — man of peace as he was. His whole soul boiled with a holy indignation — it was holy because righteous. He went to Washington City, and laid the case before President Grant. A word from the Commander of the army would have precipitated the collision. He told him so, and told him that he (the President) was responsible before God for the blood that would be shed, for the people were oppressed by a tyranny that they could not and would not longer stand. That famed General never faced a more dauntless eye than that which now looked into his. The Bishop laid the whole case before the President, and told him of the resolve of his people, and that they had yielded as far as human nature could endure. The President, as became the man, gave him a hearing, told him that he himself was going out of power, but would give him letters to his incoming successor. He did so, and the Bishop presented them in person to the President-elect at his home in the West. I had the details from the Bishop's own lips; and the sequel showed his instrumentality in lifting the load from the hearts of his people, and bringing to them relief from the tyranny that oppressed them. But all this strain upon heart and mind told upon him, as it had done upon Bishop Elliott of Georgia. The springs of life gave way under the heavy pressure.

I give these few details in order that you may understand some allusions in the lines which follow, and the withering sarcasms uttered by the Bishop himself in the extract following.

"Louisiana! matron fair, with bosom bleeding,
List to the funeral wail, all other woes unheeding;
Trail all thy banners low, abase thy queenly head;
Think not of traitors now, forget thy blood was shed;
Cry low on bended knee, 'Our Wilmer's dead!'

Queen of the South! methinks I see thee kneeling,
Discrowned in dust and shame, while tears are stealing

From eyes now dulled with grief, and memories of shame
Wrought by adopted sons; but yet there is a name,
Crowned with celestial light, worthy thy fame.

Empress of States! is it not worth the telling?
Thou hadst one son — a Prince — whose voice now swelling
The antiphone of heaven, erst in his manhood's prime,
Nursing his royal heart at fountains pure, sublime,
Poured out his kingly soul for thee, like generous wine.

Mother of many creeds and nations! thou who barest
Scars of a conflict on thy regal brow, — thy best and bravest
Into the quiet grave hath passed forevermore.
The sweet persuasion of his wondrous tongue no more
Shall claim a boon for thee : his battle's o'er.

Louisiana! Mother! Queen! thou heedest not thy losing;
The fray is sharp, the conflict lengthens; and the closing
Of warrior hosts in battle shock hath stunned thine ears;
A fell disease has fouled the sweetness of thy perfumed
    airs,
But more than this is lost to thee, — a good man's prayers!

And thou, O Church of God! while sadly breathing
Funereal orisons, receive his mantle, and, his sword un-
    sheathing,
Fill up the breach, when thou a man dost find
Refreshed with childhood's grace, a warrior brave, yet
    kind,
A lion, yet a lamb, a minister to men, a man of mark and
    mind."

But let the good Bishop speak himself, as he did to his church in council assembled. It was rarely that he thus spoke, but it was when the very stones should have cried out. He was speaking of that class of men who had come to his State for plunder, who, being disturbed at their unholy work, had invoked the aid of the General Government, saying that they were interfered with in their roguery, and that the Southern people were not yet subdued.

The Bishop writes, —

"If you listen to their complaints, no cause ever had so many martyrs. Martyrs! History portrays the victims of persecution, in all ages, hiding themselves from public view, and seeking refuge in the wilderness, or in dens and caves of the earth. It has been reserved for these Southern martyrs to be clothed with political power, and to command for themselves and their adherents the highest offices of profit and dignity. Behold them ostracized from their homes to become representatives in the Legislature; pilgrims and wanderers, traversing their judicial circuits quietly and leisurely to administer justice; driven by the sharp edge of persecution to occupy lordly mansions, and to sit down at sumptuous tables, — men who had never riches, and, some of them, never homes, before!

"Persecution is not very sharp which is thus displayed. Of one thing these people complain, and have a right to complain, — 'that the people under their rule are not satisfied.' No, they are not satisfied. Bereft of power in the land of their inheritance, the voice of their complaint cannot be hushed in a moment. Beholding the sad breach made in many communities and households, the deep sigh will escape from their lips, 'This is not the necessary result of emancipation.'

"For this restlessness and loud complaint, they are abused for disloyalty, and disobedience to authority. 'The South was never more proud and defiant before the war,' are the words which fell from the lips of ruling statesmen in Congress. 'Protection' is demanded from this great wrong! 'Protection!' — for those in power from those out of power. 'Protection!' — for scorpions who have stolen the dove's nest, that they shall not be obliged to hear the plaintive cries of the mother bereft of her young. 'Protection!' — for the soft slumbers of the wolf gorged with his prey, that he shall not be disturbed by the bleating of the sheep-fold upon the midnight air!

"I am bold to make this charge — not against the chief magistrate of this nation, who is often in our prayers, never in our animadversions; nor against the chief ruler of this State, to whom we are equally bound to render honor — but against the power which is stronger than both, and which is holding this State under its inexorable sway, I am bold to make this charge. Modern history has no example of a power so hard to propitiate, perhaps no example of equal patience under such misfortunes.

"Was it a mute prophecy of our coming fate, which is expressed in the emblem upon our national escutcheon, — the eagle with one talon holding forth the olive-branch of peace to all nations, and with the other grasping the arrows of death pointed to its own breast — friendly to all others, intolerant and cruel only to its own?"

There is nothing in the "Letters of Junius" finer and more withering than this sarcasm.

But read from him on another theme, — the coming final retribution. It is a very suggestive fact that the words which follow came heated with intense faith from the soul of the gentlest and sweetest nature, — one who would turn aside from crushing a worm. Yet there are no words which approach in plainness and terribleness the language used by our Lord Himself. When will Christian people turn from the streams fouled by their own imaginings, and drink the water of life fresh from the spring-head, — "The Truth"?

There is no mawkish sentimentality in Nature or Revelation, but there are in both these volumes life and death.

But let the good Bishop speak. I quote from one of his addresses to his council.

I met him shortly after this address had been published, and said to him, "You write as if you had a personal animosity against the Devil." Assuming that peculiar look of his when suddenly solemnized, he said, "Yes, I have, sir. He is the greatest enemy I have. He has done me a world of mischief. I hate him, sir."

If he so did hate, it was the only being he did hate, and that because the Adversary opposed the goodness of the good God. There was a grand piety in such hate. I wish I could give you all his words: they are much needed in this generation, which is in a condition of violent re-action from puritanic ideas of the Deity. He writes,—

"So we learn from Revelation to define the power of that malicious spirit, whose personality involves the fate of the Bible and humanity. To dispute this truth is to endanger the whole gospel. The fastidious clemency which would cover from human sight the terrors of hell and the infernal malice of Satan and his legions, had no place in His teaching. He knew, as no human teacher can know, what was the mystery of the second death, and what dark, infernal agencies crowd the avenues which lead to it; and He made it known in words which burn like fire. Three times, in as many consecutive sentences, He spoke to the multitude of the torment of damned spirits, — 'where their worm dieth not, and the fire is not quenched.'

"To contradict this testimony, or to dilute it, is to deprive religion of its august power. Mankind are not to be converted to hate sin by extinguishing its penalties. Hell is not less a reality than Heaven, is not less vividly depicted, is not less enduring, and eternal in its duration. Revelation will not be accused of exaggeration in the description which is given of the blessedness of the heavenly Jerusalem. None are willing to believe that its streets of gold, its white robes, its applauding hymns of joy, express more than is true of the felicity of the saints in light. You can no more evacuate hell of its terrors than Heaven of its beatitudes. You can no more extract the pungency from the torments of the damned than you can silence the Seraphim's song. There will nothing be left for faith, if you can wrest the Scripture to prove that torment does not mean torment, and everlasting does not mean everlasting."

Towards the close of the address, he writes, —

"I have arrived at the close of a painful demonstration, which I did not undertake without repugnance. If it shocks your sensibilities, do not think it a subject of congratulation, or any proof of superior intelligence, virtue, or refinement. Good men are sometimes betrayed into complacency with flippant allusions to this august mystery. It may silence this raillery to reflect that they are in alliance with the most degraded of their race. You are not alone, ye men of wit and levity, in dashing from your lips the 'cup of trembling.' Multitudes are convinced by your arguments. The murderer, the spoiler of innocence, the base miscreant, sunk in ignorance, clotted with vice and infamy, — their voices are in unison with yours in disowning the doctrine of eternal punishment. Your scepticism is greeted with a glad welcome in every retreat of crime, and is only strange and foreign to the innocent breast of childhood, and to the faith of holy men and martyrs in the Church of God. You may refuse to believe in hell; but, with such grim followers, you have no cause to be proud of your discernment, arching your brow contemptuously upon the ignorance and credulity of believers. . . .

"I will speak more feelingly. Until this doctrine is received and felt by you, as God reveals it in His Word, notwithstanding your professions, you are ignorant of the mystery of redemption. You are not saved, for you were never lost. The blessings of redemption will never be yours until you beseech God to break in pieces your pride, by giving you a profound view of your own misery, a lively conviction of the hatefulness and malignity of sin, and an implacable hatred of yourselves as sin has made you, so that your words may be true words, and not words of mockery, when you pray, 'From everlasting damnation, good Lord, deliver us.'

. . . "There is no danger that the Church of which we are members will not grow and increase in power with the progress of education in this country. There is no danger that a large share of the intelligence, refinement, sober morality of this land, will not be well represented in our sanctuaries. But, is there not danger that the independence and fidelity of our priesthood may be overawed by the redundance of worldly wealth, or the fastidiousness of public taste, enfeebling the tone of the pulpit? Our strength will die out when we hear no more the stern expostulations to sinners to 'flee from the wrath to come.'

"This Church has need of iron in its blood. It has need of fire in its veins, and majesty in its voice to make men feel and tremble, who are now buried in carnal sloth and security. It is quite clear that the words which go forth from our pulpits on future punishment have not the sober reality, or the vivid flash and power, to silence criticism and rebuke. No man smiles at lightning when it leaps from the clouds, and shakes its glittering spear above his head. It may not produce repentance, but it is too awful for derision. May not the fault be in our preaching, rather than in the Revelation itself, that the torments of the damned evoke words of carping criticism instead of solemn awe and trepidation? We do not stand before the people with the awe upon us of this great mystery.

"Come, ye tongues of fire which rested on the early messengers of the gospel, and burn this awful truth into the minds of ministers and people! He, Who cannot deceive, asserts it, — that the unbelievers, the profane, the careless, who are lovers of pleasure more than lovers of God, are exposed to the unknown pangs of the second death. Calmly we stand in the presence of those whose end, disguise it as we may, is eternal exclusion from the presence of God.

"The conversion of sinners, the salvation of souls, it is no enthusiasm to say, is the great work which God has delegated to His people. He might have chosen agencies more worthy, but He has not done so. The sublime task of spoiling Satan of his power, and gathering repentant sinners from threatened punishment to people the abodes of the blessed, is your work and mine; and, if not done by us, it will be left undone. Heaven throws wide its gates to animate our labors; ransomed saints are waiting to authenticate our faith; imperishable crowns to reward our fidelity.

"Alas! for that cold, mocking incredulity, which would exchange this sure inheritance of glory, pledged to every true believer, for a doubtful and precarious fate; which concerns itself rather to snatch a gleam of comfort from God's judgments, than to find safety in His promises; more intent to deprive the kingdom of darkness of its woes, than to gain an abundant entrance into 'The Everlasting Kingdom of our Lord and Saviour, Jesus Christ.'"

But I feel that I am not doing justice to the good Bishop by taking detached sentences from his writings. I merely wanted you to see the spirit of the man. I wish I could picture him as I see him. Some day I hope that some one will be found to gather up his choicest sermons and addresses for the enrichment of our Church-literature.

I will only add in conclusion, that, to all his other graces and attractions, there was an unspeakable purity and delicate refinement of nature, which permeated his whole life, and covered him as a garment. I had the sense of talking with a refined woman when holding discourse with him.

He had it from a child, and by heredity, from his father and mother. He had the most delicate appreciation of genuine wit and humor, and was full of it himself, but turned with loathing from all discourse that bordered on the vulgar, as every Christian gentleman should do — especially a clergyman. He should be unfrocked — I care not what his learning and office may be — who indulges in obscene and vulgar allusions.

Your cousin was upon one occasion at a large dining-party. After the first glass of wine, the ladies, as is their wont, left the dining-room for the parlor. The gentlemen rose, as a matter of course, until the ladies had passed out. As they settled themselves to the table again, one of the company said, " Now I can give you the anecdote which I could not do whilst the ladies were present." The bishop looked gravely upon him, and said, " Will you be so kind as to consider *me* a lady, sir?" Ladies might have been safely present the rest of that evening. Alas! alas! that so much greatness and goodness and sweetness have passed out of this ungodly and impure world.

THE LATE BISHOP ELLIOTT OF GEORGIA.

In Memoriam.

I don't know that I can give my children a more complete idea of a typical Southern gentleman and Christian Bishop, than by adding to these reminiscences a portraiture which — in 1867, shortly after the war of the States — I drew of Bishop Elliott of Georgia.

He was a Southern man, a slaveholder, and a Southern patriot of the first water. When men of the South realize, as they should, that some of the finest specimens of refined Christian character are to be found in the ranks of the Republican party in the North, and when men of the North realize, as they should, that men of like refined Christian character in the South defended, and still do defend, the original right to secede under the then existing Constitution, then may we indulge the hope that the late conflict of ideas and principles may — not be buried and forgotten, — for it was too earnest and sincere a conflict to be forgotten, — but understood. Then men will respect each other, and cease stigmatizing each other by opprobrious epithets. I never allow any man to call me a "rebel," nor do I allow him to speak in my presence, unrebuked, of a war for Constitutional right as a "Rebellion."

When one sees such men as Bishops Lee of Delaware, and Potter of Pennsylvania, on one side of a great question, and such men as Bishops Meade, Elliott, and Davis, on the opposite side, they should cease from "calling people names," as the children well designate it, and calmly consider the great lessons of the hour. One great lesson may assuredly be gleaned,— that the whole truth is many-sided; that no one man, however great and good, can see all its sides. He alone, who is "The Truth," can never err.

In the memorial sermon which follows, I have aimed to view the recent conflict of ideas from the stand-point of a Bishop of the Church, born and reared in the South, and, therefore, from the Southern view of the whole question. We have no apologies to make, but feel bound by that charity which "rejoiceth in the truth," to throw whatever of light may have been vouchsafed to us upon a subject which to some minds appears dark and mysterious.

Memorial Sermon.

"*Even so, Father: for so it seemed good in Thy sight.*" — St. Matthew xi. 26.

DEARLY beloved, a great sorrow has brought us together this day. It has devolved upon me — a stranger to almost all before me — to speak of the life and labors of your dear, departed Bishop. But yet, in the church and diocese of my brother of Georgia, and surrounded by so many hearts which beat quickly at the mention of his name, I cannot feel that I, who loved as you loved, and sorrowed when you sorrowed, can be regarded as an utter stranger. When it was suddenly announced to me that the Bishop of Georgia had died, I felt once again as I had felt in childhood, when it was told me my father was no more.

Bishop Elliott was one of the three revered Bishops who had set me apart, by the imposition of hands, to the office and work of a Bishop. He had presided as senior Bishop of the "General Council" of the Southern dioceses. His experience in the office of a Bishop had extended over a quarter of a century, and constituted him, by general acclaim, our acknowledged, as he was our official, head. He was, too, by birth, talents, and culture, our representative man — the impersonation of many cherished sentiments. All through life he had been their champion, and we looked to him to be long their vindicator and defender.

You have invited me here to deliver a discourse commemorative of his life and labors. I held the request as sacred, and yet I regretted that the duty had not devolved upon another. The task requires — besides other gifts to which

I make no pretension — a degree of acquaintance with the early and inner life of the good Bishop which I was not privileged to enjoy. One cannot speak of another, as your Bishop should be spoken of, unless he can speak "that which he knows, and testify to that which he has seen."

It will be the grateful task of some intimate friend of the bishop of Georgia to gather together the reminiscences of his boyhood — those precious treasures which mothers are wont to lay up in their hearts.

A life so bright as his must needs have had an auspicious morning. It will be the duty of another to tell the Church of his early struggles, when, turning from all the dreams of youth and the blandishments of life, he gave himself, a living sacrifice, to God, and laid upon His altar the homage of his heart and all the wealth of his nature. A bright earthly future stood before the young aspirant; fond expectations were cherished of his early fame; but he turned from them all. Their light was quenched in that brighter light which met him on the way, melted his soul in penitence, and resolved for him the great question of life, "Lord, what wilt Thou have me to do?"

An account of what he was in the earlier years of his ministry we have now no longer to look for. The Alumni of his *Alma Mater* have given to us in that memoir, adopted and recently published by them, the most exquisite and truthful delineation of the man, the chaplain, and the professor. No more affectionate and graceful tribute will ever be paid to his memory.

It is, then, much to be desired that some masterhand shall take the different views presented of this great man, shall group them, and give to the Church a full-size portrait of the first Bishop of Georgia. Let this be done by no inferior hand. It should be such a portraiture as will go down to posterity with those of our other Bishops, that our children may learn to know and reverence the men who lived and labored in the early days of the Church in America.

I have proposed to myself to-day the grateful though melancholy task of speaking of the deceased as a Bishop of the Church, and, particularly, in his relations to the great subjects which have agitated this country during the few last eventful years.

When consecrated to the episcopate of Georgia, in 1841, Bishop Elliott, although young in years and in office, very soon took high rank among his brethren. He possessed in an eminent degree many of the qualities which fit men to be leaders and commanders among the people. His form was beautiful and manly, and his whole presence majestic and imposing. His manners were refined and dignified, yet kind and conciliating. His intellect was large and highly cultivated, and his views elevated and comprehensive. His disposition was ingenuous and affectionate, and calculated to win upon the affections of others. His knowledge of his fellow-men was intuitive and profound, and his forbearance with their infirmities almost exhaustless. To a disposition ever ready to give way in matters of trifling importance, he united a strength of conviction and a firmness of purpose which would not yield one iota of principle; and when roused to vindicate his convictions, he would at times assert them with a vehemence that was well-nigh overwhelming. So noble were his instincts, that you always knew where to find him, — if not agreed with others, yet agreeing and consistent with himself. A steady, brave, and true man he was, and so precious to the Church that he was loved and is mourned by all who seek her peace and prosperity. All these qualities marked him out as a leader among men. But yet he could never have been the leader of a party, for he sought the truth rather than victory. His views were so large that they embraced the truths held by both parties of the Church; and he was found acting with the one or the other, indifferently, as in their movements they came within the sphere of his convictions. He could not have organized a party, but he could have led a nation. He could not have drilled a caucus, but he electrified a people. Some of his thoughts, to which he knew how to give such grand expression, will never be forgotten by the men of this generation; and to this hour our hearts thrill at their recollection. His experience in the early years of his episcopate differs in no material respect from that of other Bishops in new dioceses. He found in Georgia a handful of clergymen, and some few scattered members of the Church, — not so many as he left at the time of his death in the single congregation of Christ Church, Savannah. About seven clergymen and three hundred communicants constituted the strength of the Church in Georgia, — a State embracing an area of fifty-eight thousand square miles. Over this extended tract of country he had the oversight and jurisdiction. The task was one calculated to test the most sanguine temperament. Besides the hindrances which all meet with who preach the gospel of Christ, — the innate depravity and the carnal mind, — he was called upon to commend the usages of the Church to a people who viewed with impatience, if not with sternness, every thing that savored of ceremonial observance.

The decent and comely robes of office, the gravity and solemnity of the ritual, the due subordination and reverent demeanor, were all matters of derision to a people accustomed to the free and easy mode of extemporaneous performances. At this day, when the tastes of people are setting, perhaps, too indiscriminately in an opposite direction, it will be difficult to conceive of the intense opposition to the usages of the Church at the time to which I refer.

The plan of operations which Bishop Elliott proposed to himself, in view of the magnitude of the work in hand, was to begin by establishing strong central points in every quarter of the diocese, and in course of time to work out from these centres into the surrounding rural districts. In addition to his episcopal labors, he took upon himself the charge of a church in Savannah, thus adding the cares of a pastor to the laborious work of a Bishop — an experiment, I hope, not to be repeated. At an early day, however, he turned his attention to the education of the young, and gave up his charge at Savannah to take charge of the Female Institute at Montpelier. It will be the pleasing task of the future biographer to trace out in detail the particulars of Bishop Elliott's connection with the Institute at Montpelier. I make the declaration, however, — and his biography will supply the proof, — that his whole course in connection with the Institute at Montpelier was dictated by a spirit so noble and self-sacrificing that he placed himself above the comprehension of ordinary minds. Men cannot well conceive of the existence of motives so much raised above the ordinary level. Bishop Elliott took hold of that enterprise, and invited upon himself the full responsibility of all its load of debt, with much the same spirit that one would volunteer to embark upon, and take command of, a sinking ship. Through what trial and suffering, and clouds of misapprehension, he was called to pass, few know, — only God, who knoweth all things, and the true woman whose heart shared all his solicitudes. He was not bound to undertake the responsibility by any legal obligation whatsoever. The debts contracted before his connection with the Institute were in no way binding upon him, but he felt that the honor of the Church might in some way be involved; and he determined, that, sink or swim, he would venture all upon it. And all was ventured, and all was lost save honor and the consciousness of duty attempted. According to the rules of arithmetic, it was but a sorry venture: viewed in the light of the motives which inspired him, it approached the sphere of martyrdom. Had he been less self-sacrificing, he would have obtained more credit from the world, which always looks for motives on its own level. Men could not understand how one could risk so much without some motive of ultimate gain. When that history shall have been written, and the amount of sacrifice made known, the people of Georgia will, with new surprise, understand who and what the Bishop was who taught them the great lesson of self-sacrifice. In all his intercourse with his fellow-man, he illustrated the idea of honor so delicately drawn by the hand of a master : —

> "Say, what is Honor? 'Tis the finest sense
> Of justice which the human mind can frame,
> Intent each lurking frailty to disclaim,
> And guard the way of life from all offence
> Suffered or done."

But the scheme did not turn out as he had hoped and willed. Few came to his aid; and he turned, with a heart almost broken with disappointment, to his remaining duties. It is pleasing now to learn that one of his latest acts was to lay the corner-stone of a chapel at the Montpelier Institute. The rock which supplied the material was gathered together by himself some twenty years before. It was a source of peculiar pleasure to him to witness the revival and prosperity of his much-loved school; and his face was seen to beam once more, as of old, with the light of hope and pleasure. Thus have we seen the clouds lift at sunset, and open to us a glimpse of parting day.

We come now to trace the course of the Bishop of Georgia through a stormy period in the history of this country. It becomes necessary to refer to this period, not with the view of reviving the remembrance of a past conflict, but to rescue from unmerited reproach the memory of a Bishop of the Church, whose highest aim had ever been to set forth peace and quietness among all people, and to know nothing among men save Jesus Christ and Him crucified. If he ever breathed words which savored of strife, it was that a sure and lasting peace might thereby be established, and good will more certainly prevail. Certain fanatical ideas had assumed a dangerous and threatening attitude toward the institutions of the South. Casting aside the traditions of the past, the teachings of statesmen, philosophers, and fathers, — to say nothing of the sanctions of a solemn political compact, — this pestilent heresy dared even to lay its hand upon the Ark of the Covenant, and to deny the supreme authority of the Word of God in the last appeal. It was this moral and religious feature of the movement in question which called into active opposition the clergy of the South, and forced them to become prominent in the conflict which soon ensued. They were called upon, not only to clear themselves from the imputation of a grievous crime, but — and this more deeply concerned them — to maintain the supremacy of the Word of God, and the teachings of universal tradition. Whenever there is a conflict of principles, the men will always be found who are raised up for the crisis, — prophets who discern the coming evil, and men of nerve and will to vindicate and defend the right.

Bishop Elliott stood out prominently in his sphere, and with all the ardor of his nature (as did Bishop Meade of Virginia) addressed himself to the discharge of his full duty. At an early day he had discerned the signs of the times, and foresaw, with extraordinary distinctness, the ultimate tendencies of the whole movement. It was at first a conflict of ideas, and ideas could only be met by ideas. The Bishops of the Southern dioceses, Bishop Polk taking the lead, together with divers of the clergy and laity, set themselves to the establishment of a seat of learning, to be called the "University of the South," which, it was hoped, in time, might take rank with the universities of the Old World, and become the great educator of Southern youth. It was a vital part of the plan, that this University should be placed under the entire guardianship of this our pure branch of the Catholic Church, whose faithful allegiance to God's Holy Word, and traditional reverence for catholic truth, might lend the sanctities of a sound faith to sweeten the sources of knowledge, and give a right direction to all its power.

The whole scheme was projected upon a scale commensurate with the grandeur of the design. The good Bishop and his equally zealous coadjutors have been blamed by some for the magnitude of their aims, and plan of operations, but, I think, most unjustly. Why is it that the interests of knowledge and religion do not justify the same generous expenditure that is lavished upon objects of merely material importance? Millions will be subscribed to establish, and even to shorten, lines of communication and travel. The projectors of such schemes are hailed with ovations as the benefactors of their race. It is, for the most part, only when enterprises are started which look to the interests of men's hearts and minds, that their advocates are regarded as visionary and extravagant. Is it that the worthy Bishop and his coadjutors were too grand in their aims, or that his critics were too grovelling? The truth is, the man of whom I speak to-day was a man of large proportions: he was made upon a large scale. The traditions of his house and his personal culture rendered him dissatisfied with whatever was inelegant and incomplete. Whatsoever he did, even in matters of comparatively small importance, he did with a certain nameless grace and elegance. There was in his dress and conversation, and in his correspondence, — even to the penmanship and paper, — a finish which was quite characteristic. This elegance, amounting perhaps to fastidiousness of taste, may have disqualified him for certain rough details of duty, but it eminently fitted him to take the lead in every thing that was grand and beautiful; and it is the ordination of Providence that each man shall serve in his own lot and after his own order. Never was an enterprise commenced under better auspices, and attended with more encouraging tokens of success, than the University of the South. It promised to supply a great want, and appealed to the deepest sympathies of all who could take in the magnitude of the interests involved. Bishops Polk and Elliott — twin-brothers in life, and in death not long divided — gave themselves to the personal task of canvassing the Southern States. The Southern people met their appeals for endowments with a generous response. The site was procured, the grounds were marked out, and the foundation of the building was laid. The Bishop of Vermont (Hopkins) — *clarum et venerabile nomen* — gave his invaluable counsel and presence in the preliminary work.

Such was the attitude of things when the storm, which had been so long brewing, burst forth, and the thick cloud of war settled down upon the land. The interests of this cherished University suffered peculiar loss. The fortunes which had been pledged to its erection and support were swept away; and its munificent patrons are now either exiles from their native land, or are struggling under unkindly influences for their daily bread. Even the foundation-stone, which had been laid in faith and prayer, was rudely torn from its bed, and despoiled of its sacred treasures. The object of this institution was distinct and widely known, — to educate in harmony with Southern ideas, — and upon its devoted head came the full force of the opposing element; as when the lightning consumes the shaft which vainly aims to avert its fury, and conduct it harmlessly to the ground.

Inscrutable is the will of God, that so many of man's noblest efforts should seem to be in vain, and wickedness and violence be permitted a temporary triumph. Impenetrable mysteries are these, which baffle the highest reason. Priceless blessings will they be, if they teach us to say in faith, "Even so, Father: for so it seemed good in Thy sight."

Into that mighty conflict which ensued, Bishop Elliott threw himself with all the enthusiasm of his soul; and he never disavowed his deeds, and never repented of them.

"Fortuna non mutat genus."

In this presence, and by the recent grave which should enclose, if possible, all painful and unavailing memories, it does not become me, nor have I the desire, to speak of the past in its political and sectional aspects. But it does become me, and I hold it to be my sacred duty, — a duty which he would have faithfully performed for me, — to see that no nettles shall be planted on his grave. We bury our dead, but they are not forgotten, nor shall their tombs be dishonored.

We can recall — shall we ever forget it? — those memorable discourses of the Bishop, which spoke with trumpet-tongue through this land, reviving the hearts of the fearful and desponding, reminding the people of God's wonders in the olden time, telling them how that "out of the eater came forth meat, and out of the strong came forth sweetness." Those glowing prophecies, conceived in as sublime faith as ever inspired the seers of old, were not fulfilled in the form in which they appeared to his own rapt vision. Far-seeing as man may be, God sees farther still. Great and far-reaching as may be the plans of man, they fall short of the Divine plan. God alone is great and wise and good. Poor, narrow, short-sighted man! — he lives in his little world, of which he and his loved ideas constitute the centre. Is it wonderful, then, that man, the wisest man, should be doomed to perpetual mistakes and disappointments? We propose for ourselves: God disposes for others also. We plan for a part: He arranges for the whole. The universe is the theatre of the Divine plan, and eternity alone shall give scope to the fulfilment of the vision.

Truth shall ultimately prevail, and wrong shall be put down, and justice shall be vindicated, but — and here is our common mistake — not according to our desires and judgments and purposes. Not in the forms which we have fashioned for them, but in more glorious and abiding beauty shall our buried hopes attain unto their resurrection. We believe in the resurrection of the dead, but that body which we sow is not that body that shall be; but God giveth it a body as it hath pleased Him, and to every seed his own body. It may be "sown in dishonor, it shall be raised in glory."

These are the revelations from Heaven which come to us as we stand by the graves of our loved ones, and bid us look up from the dust and dishonor, as it goes to earth and corruption, to those glorious forms in which we shall greet them on the morning of their resurrection.

It has been charged upon Bishop Elliott and upon others, that they have at times over-stepped the limits of their calling, and have brought into the pulpit, themes other than those which are given them in trust by their Master. It may be so. I am not here to speak of my brother, or any other sinful man, as faultless. One of the curses of this day and generation is the fulsome and indiscriminate eulogy which is poured forth in obituaries and funeral discourses. No wonder that the world looks upon our humbling confessions of guilt and unworthiness as cant and hypocrisy, when so much of perfection is claimed for the living and the dead. Bishops are fashioned out of men. Earthen vessels are they, to whom a heavenly treasure is intrusted. More than human would they have been, if under that tremendous pressure of feeling, the recollection of which, even now at times, causes a tightening of the chest, their thoughts had not sometimes overflowed in strong and resistless expression. The good Bishop was not more than human. Indeed, it was his humanness that constituted his peculiar charm, and attracted to him all our hearts.

There is a something, less than human, which will never offend after this manner. There is a cold-blooded indifference, which cannot be roused in holy indignation, and it may pass for great moderation; there is a time-serving timidity which shrinks from the consequences of a deed of daring, and it may pass for great prudence; there is a calculating policy which gauges all questions by the standard of profit and loss, and it will pass for great sagacity. Men of this stamp can go through the fire unharmed, because there is no material in them to be kindled. These are the less than human.

Bishop Elliott was not a man of a timid and calculating nature. He had been reared in the school of honor, whose teachings, when sublimated by the grace of God, impel men to dare all consequences in the assertion and maintenance of the right. He had not been his father's son, he had been recreant to his whole race, if, in a question of sentiment and principle, he had paused to calculate the consequences by any standard of earthly profit. It is this spirit — travestied in the code of worldly honor — which inspired the noble army of martyrs, and made them to rejoice that they were counted worthy to suffer shame and death for a cause which they honored and espoused.

When men such as these fall into error, it is after their own manner, and in the line of their own nature. They are incapable of meanness, cowardice, and treachery; but when their indignation is aroused, they are prone to overflow the bounds of moderation. Errors of this kind are wont to be found in connection with generous and impassioned temperaments. These are the infirmities which God knoweth, and, as a Father, pitieth; and, blessed be His holy name, when repented of, are, with sins of a deeper dye, washed away in the most precious blood of Christ, and remembered no more forever.

But there is something more that must be said in this connection. It happens, oftentimes, that questions of morals and religion are so closely interwoven with political ideas and events, that it is very difficult, if not quite impossible, to handle the one without touching the other. Especially is this the case when moral ideas seize upon the reins of power, and become aggressive and coercive.

Bishop Elliott had imbibed strong and distinct political ideas. They were a portion of his inheritance; they were the traditions of his race and of his house; they mingled in his nurture, and he held them with all the strength of his strong nature. Of these I shall not further speak: they belong not to this occasion, nor to the purpose of this discourse. But there was an element mingled with the recent conflict, not only of a political and social character, but one involving a great question of morals, and possessing a deep philanthropic and religious interest.

In these Southern States, there was to be found a race of people distinct in color and in social position from the ruling race. This amiable and docile people grew up with us in our houses, were our playmates in childhood, and became, in after-life, our trusted friends and dependants.

Into the secret of that tender bond, which united the two races, a stranger cannot enter. This people became gradually Christianized. Their habits of subordination to their earthly master inclined them to an easier submission to the will of God. Their obedience, once inwrought, naturally went forth to every object of reverence and authority. It would be difficult for any one to recall the instance of an infidel among them, and their submission to the will of Heaven was proverbial. All this sprang naturally from

> "The ingrained instinct of old reverence,
> The holy habit of obediency."

As the influences of Christianity continued to extend among the masters, the relation between them and their servants became less and less mercenary, and more and more patriarchal. It may be safely affirmed that there lived not upon the face of the earth a class of people, occupying the social position of our slaves, who were better cared for, and better remunerated for their labor. The Southern system had solved the most difficult question in political economy. To feed and clothe well the laborer; to take care of the children, the aged, and the sick; to prevent pauperism; to diminish blindness, muteness, and lunacy, those sure indications of physical deterioration; and to insure the steady growth of population, — has been a task too great for the political economist. It will not need to take the testimony of Southern people upon this point. The dominant party in this country do now declare — whether rightly or not, I am not now considering — that this race, just now emancipated, is not only entitled to all the privileges, but capable of discharging all the duties, of American citizenship; and yet the ancestors of this people, a few years ago, were heathen savages in the wilds of Africa. What Christian mission, in the same space of time, has accomplished the same results for any heathen nation, that have been wrought out for this people in their connection with Southern influence, at Southern firesides?

Bishop Elliott was the type of the best Southern men in all his relations to this unhappy race. Understanding, as none but a Southern man brought up with them can understand, their childlike helplessness and dependence, and believing that the maintenance of existing relations was necessary to their continued existence and well-being as a people, for time and eternity, he took his stand by their side, and strove with all his might to avert what he deemed their ruin, and became the impassioned advocate of their cause. He who cannot understand what I am now saying, cannot comprehend the man of whom I am speaking.

I do not desire to be understood as now discussing the merits of this vexed question in any form. It is practically settled, and it is to the interest of all that it should not be disturbed. But I am here to see that the memory of a great and good Bishop is vindicated, and that his prominence, in what appeared to him the cause of humanity and religion, should never be confounded with the notoriety of those men who discuss party politics when they should preach Jesus Christ. I do proclaim, and will forever maintain, that the motives of Bishop Elliott and of kindred spirits, in their efforts to perpetuate, at least for a while, the relation of master and servant, were noble, patriotic, unselfish, and Christian. He foresaw, or thought he foresaw, — which is the same thing, so far as the motive is involved, — that the sudden disruption of the bond between him and the people he loved and cared for, would surely tend to their gradual deterioration and to their ultimate extinction. He felt that it would be a frightful wrong; and he rose up like a giant in all his strength, and said, virtually, "This must not be; and, God being my helper, this shall not be." He may have been mistaken, for it is human to err. If he was, it was his infirmity, and not his fault. His whole life presents a clear record in regard to that people to whom he was bound by a thousand ties of affection, and by the tenderest remembrances of mutual service.

He cared for them in every way, and sought to bring to them all the elevating and consoling truths of the Holy Gospel. His labors were richly blessed. He saw them gathering by hundreds under the wings of the Church, and becoming partakers with him of the same altar; and his affectionate nature was gladdened by the spectacle. When the downfall came, he sorrowed most of all for the poor, unhappy beings, who, suddenly and by an unlooked-for providence, had been bereft of their wonted guardianship, and consigned to what seemed a hopeless orphanage.

Even then he ceased not to love and care for them. Hear how he speaks in his last address to his sons of the clergy: "Love must go along with it" (the work of the Church for them); "gratitude for their past services; memories of our infancy and childhood; thoughts of the glory which will accrue to us, when we shall lead these people, once our servants, but not now as servants, but above servants, as brethren beloved, and present them to Christ as our offering of repentance for what we may have failed to fulfil in the past of our trust."

But Bishop Elliott's position was peculiarly prominent in the ecclesiastical movements which took place upon the outbreak of civil war. Happily, under the protection of God's good providence, our branch of the Church in the United States had kept herself aloof from the agitation of all sectional and political questions; and her legislation, the natural outgrowth of her spirit, had been uniformly church-like and catholic. The earthly alloy of political ideas, which had disintegrated the various denominational bodies, had never entered into her legislative halls. The General Convention, which met in Richmond in 1859, will long be remembered for the Christian charity and harmony which marked all its deliberations. It was composed of clergymen and laymen from every section of the country; and yet when the first overt act of fanatical aggression took place on the northern boundary of the State of Virginia, in whose capital they were assembled, the event, which shook the whole country to its centre, did not stir a ripple upon the surface of debate. The whole movement, therefore, of the Southern dioceses, looking to a separate organization, was the result of a sheer physical necessity, as if an abyss had suddenly yawned between the two sections. We mark the recognition of this fact in the letter of the Bishops, which summoned the Southern dioceses to meet, by their deputies, in the city of Montgomery. This letter, signed by Bishops Polk and Elliott, the senior bishops of the then seceded States, distinctly states that "this necessity (for a convention of the Southern dioceses) does not arise out of any dissension which has occurred within the Church itself, not out of any dissatisfaction with either the doctrine or discipline of the Church. We rejoice to record the fact that we are to-day, as Churchmen, as truly brethren as we have ever been, and that no deed has been done, nor word uttered, which leaves a single wound rankling in the breast. We are still one in faith, in purpose, and in hope; but political changes, forced upon us by a stern necessity, have occurred, which have placed our dioceses in a position requiring consultation as to our future ecclesiastical relations."

In pursuance of this call, deputies from some of the Southern dioceses met together, first at Montgomery, held an adjourned session in the ensuing autumn at Columbia, and there framed the constitution and canons which subsequently became the laws of the "General Council of the Church in the Southern States." In all the preliminary proceedings, Bishop Elliott took a leading part, and showed himself a master of assemblies. It is pleasing now to recall the exquisite tact with which he guided the deliberations of the house to the end proposed; how patient he was of opposition, how respectful he was to the opinions of others, how easy to compromise in matters indifferent, and how unbending and intensely in earnest when asserting the truth and right. It is difficult to conceive any thing finer than his whole bearing. It has left upon the mind the impression that is left by a beautiful dream, — alas, too soon vanished! When we look at the results of this legislation, we see but little to mark the difference between the constitution and canons of the General Convention and those of the General Council. But this was the important end attained, — that there was so little of change effected, where the opportunity for change was so boundless. The result is given by Bishop Elliott himself, with characteristic felicity, in the Pastoral of the General Council. "The Constitution is the same as that of the Church from which we have been providentially separated, save that we have introduced into it a germ of expansion which was wanting in the old Constitution." "The Canon law is the same moderate, just, and equal body of ecclesiastical law by which the Church has been governed on this continent since her reception from the Church of England of the treasures of an Apostolic ministry and a liturgical form of worship." Upon the death of Bishop Meade, — that true and brave old Bishop, whose very name is a tower of strength, — Bishop Elliott became the senior Bishop of the "General Council." The Pastoral set forth at the first session of that body was the production of his pen, and (in the language of "The Church Journal") "in elevation of tone, in dignity, force, and beauty of style, has been surpassed by no Pastoral ever issued in this country." The spirit which pervaded this Council was the self-same spirit which presided in the councils of the blessed Apostles, and they who were permitted to take part in its deliberations will ever fondly recur to its sessions as privileged beyond the ordinary assemblies of men. There was a Bishop at its head unto whom utterance had been given; and he sent forth to the world those words of peace and good will which then sounded so sweet amid the din of war, and are now so precious to us, who are gathering together these mementos of his worth and excellence. In his own glowing words, "Our first duty, therefore, as the children of God, is to send forth from this Council our greetings of love to the Churches of God all the world over. We greet them in Christ, and rejoice that they are partakers with us of all grace which is treasured up in Him. We lay down to-day before the altar of the Crucified all our burdens of sin, and offer our prayers for the Church Militant upon earth. Whatever may be their aspect towards us politically, we cannot forget that they rejoice with us in the one Lord, the one faith, the one baptism, the one God and Father of all; and we wish them God-speed in all the sacred ministries of the Church. Nothing but love is consonant with the exhibition of Christ's love which is manifested to His Church; and any note of man's bitterness, except against sin, would be a sound of discord mingling with the sweet harmonies of earth and Heaven. We rejoice in this golden cord, which binds us together in Christ our Redeemer; and like the ladder which Jacob saw in a vision, with the angels of God ascending and descending upon it, may it ever be the channel along which shall flash the Christian greetings of the children of God!"

The General Council no longer has an existence. It had fully accomplished its temporary mission in holding compactly together for a while the Southern dioceses, and in affording scope for their mutual helpfulness. When the results of war had fused the contending sections into one nationality, and after the General Convention had met and renewedly illustrated its traditional spirit, the General Council came together, released the several dioceses from their pledges of union, declared them free in good faith to renew old relations, and adjourned with the general understanding that there were no longer any sufficient grounds upon which a Churchman should desire to maintain a separate organization. I doubt if there is in history a more striking exemplification of the working of the true Church spirit than is to be found in the records of the two ecclesiastical bodies which met at Philadelphia and Augusta in the autumn of 1865.

I dwell at this time upon this period in the history of the Church, because the life of Bishop Elliott occupies a conspicuous place in the history of the whole movement, and because there are many who have misconceived, and in some instances have misrepresented, the motives by which he was actuated. He was one of the two Bishops who called together the Southern dioceses in council; and he it was, who, at a later period, set forth most emphatically the terms deemed essential to re-union. The General Council had performed certain acts, and those acts, he said, must be ratified. They were so ratified. There were no concessions made on either side, and none were asked. There was no occasion for the display of magnanimity, in the ordinary acceptation of the term. The course pursued by both parties was sensible, right, and churchlike. The wound, if there was any, healed, as in all healthy bodies it will, by first intention. I have spoken with confidence of Bishop Elliott's course and motives during this period of his life, because I know whereof I affirm, and because it was during this period that I first made his intimate acquaintance. We felt and thought and acted together. Together we resolved to meet our brethren in General Council, and to be governed as circumstances might direct — if it should seem best — to undo our work with the same deliberation with which it had been done, and with what we deemed to be a due regard to the interests of all concerned. And I may mention here, as illustrative of the Bishop's character, that when, having all things in readiness to declare the accession of his diocese to the

General Convention, he found that the sister diocese of Alabama was suffering from a military intrusion, he took no step until advised that the intrusion had been withdrawn, and that the diocese was free to act in concert with his own. So true to nobleness were all his instincts. Some zealous and overheated minds have expressed surprise that Bishop Elliott and some others should have consented to a re-union of the Church. But they neither comprehended the man nor the spirit of the Church. It had been an easy task for him to have led a separate party, and he might thereby have gained a transient popularity. But he had higher aims. He loved the Church of God; ay, above his chief joy, he sought her peace and prosperity; and with that sweep of vision and that largeness of soul with which he was so richly endowed, he saw that the prestige and strength of the Church could only be preserved by her reunion; and at the proper time he spoke the emphatic word which practically settled the question. I doubt much if the moment of his highest exaltation as a man and a Churchman was not the moment, when, repressing all of personal feeling, and yet yielding no conviction, and compromising no principle, he stood forth and said virtually, "The Church must close up her ranks. We are one in faith and hope — there must be no division in the body."

In referring to this action of Bishop Elliott, a writer in "The Southern Churchman" (Rev. Dr. Slaughter) most truthfully and eloquently said, —

"The whole South joins in the dirge over one of her most splendid products — her champion and her child, every pulse of whose large heart did beat in sympathy with her in her weal and woe. The whole Church should honor the memory of the man who wore the mitre so becomingly; 'who was so pure in his vocation that his virtues did plead his cause' like angels trumpet-tongued; the man who, though born and ripened under a Southern sun, with all the fervor of a Southern man's affections, instincts, and prejudices, at a critical moment hushed them into silence, and came forward, and laid them upon the altar of a bleeding Church to heal her wounds."

I met with Bishop Elliott for the last time at the General Council in the autumn of 1865. Great changes had taken place. His fondest earthly hopes had been crushed, and his most sanguine predictions had been unfulfilled. He bore it all as became him. Strength and greatness never seem so attractive as when chastened by heavy affliction. Sorrow gives that softness of coloring which the painter is wont to use in his last touches when toning down the picture. There was the same winning smile, the same loving recognition, but withal, there was an undertone of indescribable tenderness which bespoke a great sorrow encountered and endured. The thought prominent in his mind was duty to the Church; and he it was, who, in his closing address to the Council, — never written, and, alas! now no longer to be recalled, — gave expression to it. "We should ask" — thus ran the tenor of his discourse — "not what will gratify our pride, and please the world, but what the interests of the Church demand, and what Christ would have us to do." This selfsame spirit pervaded the action of the General Convention, which had closed its session a few weeks before at Philadelphia.

The blessed Spirit of God, the Holy Comforter, in answer to the prayers of the faithful, was moving upon the heart of the Church, — deep calling unto deep under the impulse of His mysterious power, — and the waters flowed together as do the waves of the sea which a passing vessel has for the moment parted asunder.

There is nothing upon this earth so beautiful as the spectacle of an heroic soul struggling manfully with adversity, yielding at last to manifest destiny, and bowing to the divine will in unquestioning submission. There are faithful men in these latter days, who have illustrated their faith by sacrifices greater even than that which the patriarch Abraham was preparing to make upon the mount. There are some things dearer to a man than the life of his child, and when sacrificed at the divine command, through faith, are most precious offerings in the sight of Heaven.

It was one of my first thoughts, when I realized that all was over, "How does Bishop Elliott bear all this?" so long and so thoroughly identified had he been with that cause for which we were hoping and struggling. He bore it all most beautifully, as the permissive will of God without which not even a sparrow falleth to the ground. The faith which had waxed so strong in the time of action, rose to sublimity in the hour of submission. Most worthily did his demeanor illustrate the motto upon his official seal: "*In utrumque paratus agere et pati.*" Mysterious indeed to all of us were the providences of that hour, but what room for faith, if sight and reason had not altogether failed! It should be our delight to lose ourselves in the depths of the divine mysteries, because in the darkness and cloud God dwelleth, and there His children find Him. Thanks be to God that we have a Father so wise that we cannot always comprehend His ways, and so good that we can never distrust His love.

"Here bring your wounded hearts; here tell your anguish;
Earth has no sorrow that Heaven cannot heal."

Not by the power of reason do we solve divine mysteries, and turn all our sadness into rejoicing, but by the application of faith. "Even so, Father: for so it seemed good in Thy sight."

I little thought when I parted from the bishop, that I should see his face no more. His appearance gave promise of long-continued life. Time and suffering seemed to have made no serious impression on his vigorous frame, and there was no apparent abatement of his mental powers. But one is never the same after passing under a great pressure. The spring of life, when not broken, is always weakened by the strain. The grief which is denied outward expression, will flow back upon the heart, and in time will break it. He went about his work quietly and submissively, with the earnest purpose to do what yet remained to be done, but it was under circumstances of peculiar painfulness to a spirit like his. The rude tempest of war had swept through the bounds of his diocese, from the mountains to the seashore. He could not travel without seeing the marks of its violence, not only upon the devastated fields and burned cities, but upon dismantled and desecrated churches, "the abomination of desolation standing where it ought not." From every quarter of his diocese, from vacated churches and impoverished people, there came to him the cry for aid and counsel; and there was everywhere, too, to be heard that saddest lament of all, the cry of the orphan and the widow. To what straits the Southern Bishops have been driven in attempting to heed these cries, God and themselves only know. Is it any wonder that the pressure has proved too great for brain and heart?

It seems to us as if the death of our beloved Bishop had been premature, and that the tale of life had been cut short before it was all told, and a pity, too, when it was so beautiful in the telling. But we must learn to measure life, not so much by its length of continuance, as by the amount of work accomplished. Men who work hard will compress into threescore years what might have been, with less intensity, extended over the allotted threescore years and ten. It was enough that his Master was satisfied with his day's work, and that he was called to rest before the sun went down.

> "No ominous hour
> Knocks at his door with tidings of mishap;
> Far off is he, above desire and fear;
> No more submitted to the change and chance
> Of the unsteady planets. Oh, 'tis well
> With him! but who knows what the coming hour,
> Veiled in thick darkness, brings for us?"

Amid all his trials he had enjoyed a large share of life's blessings. He had been permitted to preach the unsearchable riches of the great Redeemer in Whom he trusted. He had received honor from all honorable men. Earth, and Heaven upon earth, confers no greater honor upon man than to clothe him with the office of an ambassador for Christ in the highest ministry of the Church. He had lived to see his diocese grow up under his administration, and becoming strong in all the great centres, where men most do congregate. He was spared to see his children grown up around him, and the promises of God fulfilled towards them. This life had lost many of its attractions, and the gladdening dreams of youth had all fled from him. A new order of affairs, alien from his sympathies, was in progress around him. The present condition of things was dark, and in the future no rift in the clouds was discernible. The little flocks of his servants, which he had tended with a shepherd's care, had been scattered, and came not, as of old, to his familiar call. The companions of his childhood had left him, and the trusted friends of his early manhood had nearly all preceded him, and in the place of departed spirits were waiting to welcome him. Life was not what it had been to him — the same divine mission indeed, the same call to duty, the same struggle; but it was a lone struggle. Meade, Cobbs, Otey, Polk, Rutledge, — all had left him;

and the heart of a loving man feels sadly the need of loving hearts around him. Is it to be wondered at that he was weary, and ready, like a tired child, to lie down and rest? In his own words, delivered at the burial of his brother Cobbs, the late bishop of Alabama, he exclaimed, — and what a grateful significance his words have for us now! — "Oh, the sweetness of that word '*rest!*' To cease from all the weariness of life; to be done with its cares, its perplexities, its sorrows, its miseries; to have fought the good fight of faith, and ended the struggle; to have finished the work which God has given us to do, and now to lie down and be at peace."

All ended as he would have ordered it. Before the years had come wherein men find no pleasure; while yet the keepers of the house trembled not, nor those that looked out of the windows were darkened; in the full possession of all his powers; in the bosom of his family; spared the lingering sickness and the painful parting, — he gave up the ghost, and was gathered to his fathers. Wife and children gather around the closing scene: hosts of friends crowd the procession, and even the stranger is borne unwittingly along by the swelling throng. The loving arms of beloved servants, whom he had so long and lovingly borne upon his heart, bore his precious remains to their resting-place. Amid the scenes so dear to him, by the banks of the gentle Savannah, and under the skies which had looked down upon his nativity; upon the holy festival of Christmas Day, amid anthems of Glory to God, and Peace upon Earth, — he was laid in his place of rest. It is very sad to us who are left behind, but we have no tears of bitterness to shed for ourselves when the gain to him is so incalculable. "Even so, Father: for so it seemed good in Thy sight." And for all Thy goodness and mercy to this our friend, brother, father, "We praise Thee, we bless Thee, we worship Thee, we glorify Thee, we give thanks to Thee for Thy great glory, O Lord God, Heavenly King, God the Father Almighty!"

Since writing the above, and preparing it for the press, I have heard an incident so characteristic of Bishop Elliott's nobleness of soul, that I cannot refrain from recording and perpetuating it in these "Reminiscences."

It has passed into history that the chief man of the "Confederacy" was captured, and imprisoned in the Fortress of Monroe to await trial for treason. That prison-life of Mr. Davis, with all its needless horrors and humiliations, has left a foul blot upon the history of that day. Those months of solitary imprisonment; his feeble body loaded with chains; that eye of the jailer ever fixed upon the prisoner's every motion, even in his devotions to the Most High, — what a picture of wanton insult! We, Southern people, are a forgiving people, for every true Southern man felt himself insulted in the person of his representative head. A man can be imprisoned, tried, convicted, and executed, and yet not insulted. The treatment of Jefferson Davis was a foul wrong, and we all felt it as a personal dishonor.

While the unhappy, but unsubdued, captive sat there in his lonely cell and chains, — for a long time forbidden to see even his priest, — Bishop Elliott importuned the authorities to be allowed to share the imprisonment of his chief — volunteered to partake of all its horrors. Glorious Elliott! such men redeem the character of the human race. Nor was the good Bishop alone in this sentiment. The vast Fortress of Monroe was all too small to enclose the crowd which would have sprung forward to emulate his spirit. If such men be traitors, I can only say, —

"Sit mea anima cum illis."

We of the South have not yet been schooled to enroll John Brown among "The noble army of martyrs." The roll of the South records the names of quite other men. With these we have lived, and with these we hope to share eternity. For one, I have no higher aspiration; for my posterity I ask of Heaven no richer boon.

REMINISCENCES OF THE RIGHT REV. NICHOLAS HAMNER COBBS, D.D.,

The First Bishop of the Diocese of Alabama, the "George Herbert" of the Church in America.

THIS volume would be most incomplete unless it contained some remembrance of one who had been my intimate friend for a long period of my life, and also my immediate predecessor in the bishopric of Alabama.

I hardly know how to describe Bishop Cobbs; for he was a man, in some respects, altogether unlike all other men whom I have known in character, and in the exercise of his holy office. We have had many distinguished, learned, and eloquent men in the American Episcopate, but only one Bishop Cobbs. He was the very impersonation of some of the most striking qualities of a Bishop. He looked the representative of his Lord in the sweetness, gentleness, and humility of his bearing towards his fellow-men. It required the exercise of no great imaginative power to picture him leaning on his Master's breast, and finding all his strength and solace there. He looked as if

one of the Apostles whom Christ had chosen to follow Him in His solitary sojourn upon earth. I remember now a remark of a good Methodist brother, who had had some worrying controversies about the "Apostolical Succession." I introduced him to Bishop Cobbs on one occasion; and when the Bishop left us, my good brother turned to me, and said, "I have no doubts on my mind now, for I have seen the 'Apostolic Succession.'"

Above all other men was he an humble man: alone of all other men, he embodied the spirit of meekness. I have mingled much with my fellow-men, and have observed them with much attention; and I record here what I have often remarked, "that Bishop Cobbs was the only real meek man I ever knew." I have seen earnest men, pious men, self-sacrificing men, very humble men; but I have only seen one very meek man,— a man who could take a slight or offence from his fellow-men without exhibiting passion or resentment. This is the rarest gem in the diadem of saints, and it shone serenely on his brow.

I remember just now a very characteristic incident, illustrative of his spirit of meekness. The Bishop, then Mr. Cobbs, was, at the time referred to, the chaplain of the University of Virginia,— the first chaplain that had ever ministered within its walls. It will be remembered that the University of Virginia, at its inception, did not officially recognize Christianity as one of the forces which should enter into the work of education. Indeed, there was an atmosphere of infidelity about the "Old Dominion" at that period, which poisoned even the sources of knowledge. The University was equipped by the diligence of Jefferson with all that was most advanced in the schools of learning, but Christ was not acknowledged there in the presence of any ambassador. Under a very peculiar train of events, which are well known, and need not to be repeated here, Mr. Cobbs was chosen to be the first chaplain. His modest and retiring manner, his low estimate of his own ability, in which no one agreed with him, all seemed to unfit him to cope with the spirit that held sway at the University. But how little can men judge of the spiritual forces which a man of God, imbued with the love of Christ, can bring to bear upon the hearts of his fellow-men. His very presence disarmed all opposition, and his simple telling of the wondrous old story of the love of Christ won many hearts for his dear Master.

But to the incident. He was dining out on one occasion in the vicinity of the University. At the table was one of the students, who amused himself, and thought he was amusing others, by jokes upon the clerical profession. Mr. Cobbs said not a word, and showed no sign of displeasure. As the company were about to rise from the table, he went up to the young man, and, taking his hand in a friendly manner, said, "My young friend, I am greatly obliged to you for your admonitions. We of the clergy seldom have the privilege of having our faults told us so plainly, and I trust that I shall profit by your discourse." You may imagine the discomfiture of the youth. He yielded him his homage on the spot, and became, as did all the students and professors, his devoted friend and admirer.

Is not this one of the manifold ways in which the beatitude to "the meek" is fulfilled — "they shall inherit the earth"? What is there on the earth so precious as the love and esteem of the good? what accumulation of earthly treasure can be placed in the scale with the wealth of affection which the good man lays up? Indeed, I know not which one of the beatitudes the good Bishop did not have a share in. He was "pure in heart;" he was a "peacemaker;" he "hungered and thirsted after righteousness." What fulness of joy and blessedness await the dear man on that day when his Lord from His throne shall issue His invitation, "Come, ye blessed of My Father!" His humility was as conspicuous as his meekness. He loved to preach on the text, "Be ye clothed with humility." After having announced his text, he might have sat down, for the people had the sermon exemplified in full view before them.

Mr. Cobbs was succeeded in the chaplaincy by a man of rare talent for oratory. I asked one of the professors how he liked the new chaplain. His reply was, "Mr. Cobbs's presence in the pulpit is more eloquent to me than all the flashings of oratory."

His sagacity was very remarkable, his intuitive knowledge of men was profound, and his mode of dealing with all varieties of character inimitable. We were thrown much together in the early part of my ministry, and we often held "associations" together. When I had a particularly hard case to deal with, I always invoked his aid — never, I think, without success. I loved to watch the play of his conversation, like that of a skilful angler. It was a beautiful study. Christ had indeed made him a "fisher of men." As to the dear women, they ran into his open net. Ah! how many hearts in old Bedford County, the place of his birth and earliest ministry; in Petersburg, where he gathered such a harvest of souls; in Alabama, where he carried warmth and light into every nook and corner of the State, — how many hearts in all these fields of labor do still beat with love and gratitude at the sound of his name! Such men never die, and thus, too, "inherit the earth."

His administration of his diocese was, of course, in perfect keeping with the man: he was the servant of servants, as was his dear Master, and ready to lay down — as indeed he did — his life for the flock. He gathered to him by elective affinity, a ministry like-minded with himself, and made the diocese of Alabama — what I trust it will ever be — a haven of repose for those who seek rest from the strife of faction and party.

He was a Churchman all through and through. It seemed to saturate him: it breathed in his breath, it spoke in his speech, it lived in his life. He loved his "mother," as he was wont to call her, and he spoke of her with a filial unction which cannot be described. The dear Bishop Lay, whose voice, alas! is no longer heard, and whose pen writes no more, gathered his inspiration at the feet of Bishop Cobbs. Their mutual love and admiration are indescribable; and, oh! often have I journeyed with them, and enjoyed their discourse and mutual love.[1]

With all this high appreciation of the Church, — and he loved the Church because she was Christ's, — he had a kind word and a kind thought

---

[1] After the death of Bishop Cobbs, Bishop Lay published in the Church Review a highly appreciative sketch of him.

for all that named the Sacred Name. Indeed, he seemed incapable of aught but love.

My own relations to him were peculiar, and our intimacy very close, notwithstanding our very different temperaments. He often told me that the first man who came to him after his ordination as deacon, and threw his arms around him, and bade him be of good cheer, was my father, and that his heart went forth to every one that bore the name of "Wilmer." It was in part for this reason, I suppose, that I was called to take his place in every position that he ever held in the Church. (I only succeeded him in Bedford and Alabama.) Thus have I ever been in his path, and have learned to know his footprints. They have ever pointed in the direction of duty. God grant me some of the grace that guided and sanctified his life.

His death was marked by a striking coincidence. He loved his country, as became his loyal heart. He saw the gathering of the storm of war at his very door. He had loved the Union with a deep devotion, as did all men of his class; and the idea of its dissolution was more than his frame, enfeebled by long disease, could bear. At the booming of the cannon which announced the separation of his State from the Union, his gentle spirit took its flight. His tender heart could not have borne the horrors of that dreadful war, and he was taken in out of the storm.

I would have dwelt longer upon the public life and administration of Bishop Cobbs, if I had the time and materials at hand. Most happily, the Rev. Dr. Cushman has preserved the memorial sermon ("The Israelite without Guile"), which, by request of the diocese of Alabama, he preached after the Bishop's death. The selection of the preacher for the occasion was a very wise one; for the Doctor was fitted by culture, and capability of appreciation, and by his ardent affection, to give us the likeness of the first Bishop of Alabama. I give the following extracts, and end this reminiscence with the Bishop's "parting words."

EXTRACTS FROM THE SERMON OF THE REV. DR. CUSHMAN.

"When was a subject more worthy of a tribute than the man of God whose life and death we now commemorate, the Israelite without guile? when one to whom could better be applied the testimonies of inspiration to the perfection of the saints? Did Abraham talk with God on the plains of Mamre, did Enoch walk with Him? What was their life, but like his, a life of holiness and prayer? Did the dying Jacob gather himself up in his bed, and, leaning upon the top of his staff, bless his children? Suffer us, a moment, to unveil the sacred secrets of yonder chamber of death. There lay the aged father and Bishop, his frame wasted, his strength exhausted, by months of painful suffering and disease. Already had he entered into the dark valley and shadow of death. But he could not die without once more beholding the children of his love: with them, and with the wife of his youth, he must break the sacramental bread. They are gathered from far, — his daughters, his sons, his sons-in-law, and their wives with them. In a kind providence, no living child was missing. Together they knelt around that sacred bed, together they all partook of that last sacrament, — all save one, whose tender years precluded; and when, leaning upon his elbow, the aged father raised his attenuated hand, and invoked the blessing of Heaven, the peace of God, which passeth all understanding, fell sweetly upon his own soul. He realized the truth of the promise that the righteous should not be forsaken, and that his seed should not in vain beg their bread, — the bread of heaven; and, with gushing tears of thankful joy, he could exclaim, 'Behold, Lord, here am I, and those that thou hast given me.' It was a scene which might well remind us of dying patriarchs. Not afar off did he resemble those elder saints. Like David, a man after God's own heart; like Daniel, a man of prayer; like

Nathaniel, an Israelite without guile; like St. John, full of tenderness and love; like St. Stephen, a good man, and full of the Holy Ghost, and of faith, he might well have feared the woe, denounced by our Lord when all men speak well of thee, had not, as in the case of the prophet, occasion been taken to find fault with him concerning the Lord his God. He contended valiantly for Christ, and won the universal meed of praise. He contended no less for the Church, the body of Christ; and he, who never had in his heart a thought of party enmity and strife, incurred partisan censure and reproach.

"He was a man of God from his youth; and the whole course of his life did but develop and mature those natural germs of character which were made perfect by grace. As in the sainted Griswold, it was difficult to say in him where nature ended and where grace began, so happily were they combined: and if he was thought ever to set an undue value upon the baptism and catechetical instruction of the Church, it was because he felt himself so much their debtor; because, like Timothy, by his mother and grandmother he had been early trained in wisdom's ways. The seeds were thus implanted which in after-years produced so abundant a harvest of good to himself and the Church. Impressions were thus made which no adverse influences ever impaired or destroyed. It was to these two facts, — his baptism and his catechetical training, — that he himself attributed, under God, his life as a Christian minister and bishop.

. . . .

"Bishop Cobbs was never a man to make a display of his reading and learning. His ambition never ran in that direction; but to his friends, to those who were admitted to his familiar converse, and to whom he brought out treasures new and old, he appeared, as he truly was, not only a Christian bishop, but a scholar and a learned divine. His zeal and industry atoned for his want of early opportunities; and in the classics, in English theology, in Church history, and in patristic lore, he was no mean proficient. Never man rated higher the value of learning, no one labored more to raise its drooping standard in our land. If, in these later days, he was the earnest and unfailing advocate of our own great University of the South, it was because he saw in it the realization of his hopes and dreams; because there he believed the twin-sisters, Religion and Learning, were to walk hand in hand, until they attained such fulness of stature as the world had not yet seen.

"It was amid such toil and such recreation, a

teacher by day, and a painful student by night, that Bishop Cobbs passed his earliest years. Soon he found pressing upon him the great question of his vocation in life. From early youth, influences alien to the Church had surrounded him. The Church herself, in her depressed condition, cast down, but not destroyed, could offer but little inducement to a worldly mind : for ambition, she had no glittering prize. To share her lot, to take part in her ministry, was to share her poverty and reproach. To lead such a forlorn hope required no little heroism. The question, however, was soon settled. If there was ever a doubt in his mind, which we neither affirm nor deny, it was determined without long debate for the faith in which he had been baptized, for the Church in Virginia, which, however fallen and decayed, was still the Church of Christ. In 1824 we find him at Staunton, applying to be admitted to the holy order of deacons. He had yet to be confirmed, and partake of his first communion : but once before, we believe, had he witnessed the service of the Church. Such, however, was his spotless character, such the testimonials he bore from neighbors and friends, such the necessities of the Church in Virginia, — the very application was the best proof of the sincere and self-denying piety of the applicant, — that all technical considerations were overruled. He was ordained deacon by the Right Rev. Bishop Moore, in Trinity Church, Staunton, May 23, 1824, and the same day was confirmed, and for the first time communed.

. . . .

"It was during these laborious years of parochial life that those conservative and sound views of the Church, in the profession of which Bishop Cobbs afterwards lived and died, were developed and matured. He had imbibed them from the fountain-head, from the great exponents of the English Church, and from the Word of God. The adverse influences which surrounded him had, it may be, for a while kept them in abeyance; and it was not until the experience of parish life had taught him that the truest practice can only be combined with the truest theory, that they assumed their normal place in his mind and heart. To preach Christ was his first duty, as it was his chief pleasure; to preach the Church was a duty no less. They were parts of one whole; and the question did not, could not, rise in his mind which of the two he should forbear to press. His office was to proclaim the whole counsel of God. It was not only duty: even in Bedford, he believed it policy. In the field of labor in which God had placed him, amid the diversities of heresy and schism, with multiplying sects on every side, necessity constrained him to set forth plainly and distinctly the Divine origin and Apostolic claims of 'the sect everywhere spoken against.'

. . . .

"The trumpet, we think, gives no uncertain sound. These views so announced, his views upon the sacraments, and especially upon baptismal regeneration, in the belief of which he stood side by side with Bishop Moore; his thorough reception of the doctrine of the Apostolic Succession; his later attempts at Petersburg to revive the long disused holy days of the Church; his acknowledged teachings in the pulpit and in private, — furnish all the proof we need, that, as a Churchman, he was an Israelite without guile. Bishop Cobbs was never one to stir up controversy and strife. In his unaffected humility, in his gentleness, and love of peace, he never, unnecessarily, obtruded adverse opinions upon the attention of others. He was not a man of positive assertions; he rather hinted than expressed a difference; he dwelt in social converse upon points of harmony and union. To some, he might seem to waver and to yield, when no rock was firmer. It was so in all things. In all his intercourse with his clergy, in his Episcopal addresses, in converse with a vain student, an aged servant, a brother Bishop, the same characteristic appears, the same Christian modesty spake from his tongue. Dogmatism was no element of his character. When other men affirmed, he perhaps would speak by interrogation; but his question implied no less certainty than their solemn oaths. He was not arrogant, opinionative, positive; but he was firm and decided. Let principle be involved, and no appliances could move him. We repeat, the trumpet gave no uncertain sound. The views of the Church, and of her doctrines, learned by painful study in the Word of God and the Book of Prayer, and confirmed by the experience of a parish priest, which had gradually and surely matured in the earlier years of his ministry, were the rule of his life, as they were among his chief consolations in death.

. . . .

"But the time had come when Bishop Cobbs must bid farewell to his first, perhaps his best-loved, field of labor. He must turn his back upon those Peaks of Otter, in whose shadow, as he was born, so he had hoped to live and die. There he had passed his early years, there he had labored, and seen the fruits of his labor: where once were none, a hundred communicants now kneeled. He had twined himself around the hearts of that people with cords of love that no change of time or circumstance could sunder. With spontaneous affection, they loved him in word and deed; and a farm of two thousand dollars' value was, in part, their thank-offering for the sacrifices he had made. His very presence brought to them comfort and joy and protection, and they felt safer for seeing the man of God pass daily by. It was the Divine will they must give him up, but it could only be with streaming eyes and breaking hearts. Their love could know no diminution. Other men might occupy: it was still his parish. To them always the Bishop of Alabama was the Priest of Bedford. What a scene was that when he visited the home of his nativity, a Bishop in the Church of God; when he laid his hands, first upon the eldest daughter of his heart and love, now, we trust, a saint in heaven, and then upon the aged father, who had waited thus long for the consolation of Israel. It was a time of mingled sorrow and joy. The young men wept; the strong men bowed themselves; the mothers and daughters in Israel would have gladly given themselves to him, who had sacrificed so much for them. Our own eyes fill with tears, the pen falls from our hand; and we can only say, 'If he was much worthy, Bedford loved much.'

. . . .

"Bishop Cobbs had served for fifteen years in the General Convention of the Church as one of the clerical deputies from the Diocese of Virginia.

In 1841, members of the Church, emigrants to Texas, then an independent republic, had applied to the Church in the United States to send them a Bishop. It was a post of very great responsibility and importance. The House of Bishops, zealous ever for the extension of the Church, were forward to comply with the request; and Bishop Cobbs was by them nominated as a suitable person to enter upon that great field. From motives of policy and expediency, the House of Clerical and Lay Deputies declined to unite in the preliminary action of the House of Bishops; and, to his great relief and joy, the name of Bishop Cobbs was not sent down to them for confirmation. Pending that matter, he underwent much trouble and distress lest the stern mandate of duty should call him, in the acceptance of that post, to the sacrifice, as it would then have been, of his native land. His nomination was in every way honorable; but such was his shrinking modesty and self-abnegation, that to members of his own immediate family, singular as it may seem, the knowledge of it has only come from other sources since his death. He was never the trumpeter of his own fame.

"It was in 1843 that Mr. — now, by creation of Hobart College, Geneva, N.Y., Dr. — Cobbs took charge of St. Paul's Church, Cincinnati. He had hardly entered upon his duties there, when the Church in Indiana hastened to ratify the indorsement of the House of Bishops of his suitableness to be a Bishop in the Church of Christ. He was elected to that office by the clergy, and only a doubt of his acceptance of the position prevented the concurrence of the laity. Thus, happily, he was reserved for us; and in May, 1844, at Greensborough, the Church in Alabama, by unanimous vote of her clergy and laity, invited Dr. Cobbs to her episcopate.

. . . .

"He accepted the providential call, was consecrated in Philadelphia, Oct. 20, 1844, and in the month of November had already entered upon his work, his great venture of faith.

. . . .

"We notice first and foremost the extraordinary hold Bishop Cobbs had upon the affections of his people; the wonderful union and harmony which characterized all orders and degrees of men under his jurisdiction. As he went through his diocese, everywhere preaching the gospel, as well by his presence as his words, he won his way to all hearts. He intuitively inspired, not only respect, but confidence and love, as well out of as in the Church. 'That is a good man, a sincere Christian man,' was the one, universal voice. In his presence, before his lowly piety, wickedness itself stood abashed; and those who feared not God, nor regarded man, respected him. Without compromising a principle, he acquired the good will of all; and when he approached, contentions for modes of faith died away in silence. It was ever in his mind that his mission was, if possible, to live peaceably with all men. Ministers of an alien faith were his friends in life; they stood at his bedside to learn how a Christian Bishop died; they paid to his lifeless remains the last offices of friendship and love. Look to his writings, listen to his words, and he spared not to proclaim what he believed to be the counsel of God; but he made no enemies, either to the truth or to himself, because he spake the truth in love.

"But it was in the Church that our Bishop found the strongest, and to him the dearest, proofs of love. In the sixteen years of his episcopate, confidence in him never for a moment wavered, but grew stronger and stronger until the day of his death. His diocese stood around him as one man and one heart. Never was a bishop who had a stronger hold upon his clergy and laity, — it was a revered father and loving children, — never was a diocese more happily united. His will was ours: his slightest wish was to us imperative as law. His rule, which we never felt, was absolute, at the very time we sighed, that he would not rule. This, perhaps, was one of the secrets of his great influence: what he would not seek was freely given to him. Most remarkable was the proof of our perfect trust in him, — a proof without precedent in the whole history of our confederate Church, — when two years ago, by a formal vote of our Convention, as unanimous as his election was, the entire control of our Diocesan Missions was confided to his hands. It was a confidence which the Church of the diocese nobly indorsed the same year by doubling its contributions. It was then we passed the formal vote; but that vote was only the recorded expression of what had been, from the beginning, our practice. It gave him no powers which he had not, by general approbation and consent, always exercised.

. . . .

"Bishop Cobbs, in accepting the Episcopate of Alabama, did not underrate the difficulties he would have to encounter and overcome. He counted the cost before he began to build, and realized that it was a venture of faith. In large portions of the diocese, the Church was altogether unknown; in other parts, the strongest and most unfounded prejudices existed against her. Her doctrines were not understood: her practice was misrepresented. She was, they said, a cold, formal, dead Church, having but a name to live, with the form of godliness, but not the power. That ignorance was to be enlightened: that prejudice must be lived down, and overcome. Before the Church in Alabama could have any real growth, or acquire any real strength, it must prove its claims to the respect of men. It must show by living example, as well as by precept, that it was possible for a Christian man to live within its pale. Upon that one point, all her future depended. How admirably Bishop Cobbs worked out that theorem, — how, in his own person, he demonstrated that truth, and so laid the foundation of future success, — we all know. It was for him to prepare the soil, and sow the seed: to him we owe the harvest already reaped, and shall owe, in great part at least, that which is still to come. Like the Apostle, 'in journeyings often,' in protracted absence from home, in wearisome waiting upon our water-courses, in heat and cold, over roads to which even courtesy could scarce give the name, by labors that might well have exhausted more rugged men, he penetrated into every part of his large diocese, and carried with him the gospel and the Church. Says Bishop Elliott, 'He was one of the holiest men I ever met." He so wrought that all Alabama met him, and indorsed the truth; and under its influence the diocese grew and flourished.

"Bishop Cobbs was not what Latimer would call 'an unpreaching prelate.' He magnified that part of his office. It was to him an ordinance of the gospel, and he was never so much at home as when in the pulpit. After a weary journey, it was rest to him, at night, to proclaim to a handful, or to a gathered multitude, the unsearchable riches of Christ. His preaching was plain, simple, and direct. He sought no aid of ornament, he indulged in no flights of fancy, he made no vain display of learning. He preached Christ, not himself; and not himself preached Christ, but the Church through him. No one knew this distinction better than he, who was often heard to say, that the preacher in the Church of Christ was no mere man of thirty, or threescore, but a man hoary with eighteen hundred years. With a plain, Saxon style, which was all his own, — a style toned down by severe discipline from that ornate exuberance of metaphor and ornament which characterized his earlier productions, when poetry and song guided his pen, and warmed his heart, — with a peculiar delivery, he never failed to arrest attention, and to reach the heart. There have been few preachers more effective. If not an orator in the popular sense, he had one of the best elements of oratory. His sermons were realities: he believed what he said. Every word and tone and gesture bore the impress of sincerity. His sermons were brief, confined generally to a single point; and at their close, — it is the truest test of merit, — his hearers thought not of the speaker, but of themselves and their sins. They turned away, ever with the purpose of repentance and amendment in their hearts, and with its expression upon their lips. He captivated, not their intellects, but their hearts: and out of the stores of his large experience the Christian was edified and instructed, and the sinful persuaded, and eager multitudes hung upon his words; for he spake to them with the eloquence of sincerity and truth, and with the power of God.

"Bishop Cobbs was not a man ambitious of authorship: he shrank from observation with a woman's timidity. Apart from his episcopal addresses, his appearances before the public were most rare: some seven occasional sermons make up the tale. In nearly every such case, his words sank deep into the Christian heart, and in the form of tracts have been widely circulated, some of them in many editions. They were plain, pointed, practical, the fruit of ripened wisdom and long experience, and of that rare quality, common sense, which he possessed in an eminent degree. The same remark will apply to his addresses to his convention. There was not a word in them for display, no circumlocution, no sounding phrase. He seldom travelled beyond the record: he spake for Alabama, not for the world. A brief detail of his official acts, — brief, the better to conceal his immense amount of work, — a few plain, practical suggestions touching the interests of the diocese, and the analysis is complete. There was no exordium, no peroration, very seldom such a digression, as when his heart broke out into that eloquent tribute to the memory of that 'great-hearted shepherd,' Bishop Doane. But upon what concerned his diocese, what would promote its interests, we had line upon line: here he never wearied. His warnings to his clergy against pseudo-catholicity, against the errors of Rome and Geneva, against all innovations upon the ancient usages of the Church; his exhortations to combine in our preaching 'Evangelic truth with Apostolic order,' to set forth, side by side, as cardinal truths, the doctrine of justification by faith, and the importance of the sacraments and offices of the Church — the body and soul of Christ's religion, as he termed them — to proclaim everywhere, and at all times, Christ and His Church, — these still ring in our ears: may their influence never die in our hearts! Our Diocesan Missions, the subject of his last as of his first address to us; our Diocesan School;

the Religious Instruction of Servants, which had been the life-long subject of his interest; the Catechetical Training of Children; the Widow and Orphan's Society; the Endowment of the Episcopate; the due Support of the Clergy, — these were the themes upon which he dwelt, themes to him ever new, because ever interesting, because upon them our growth as a Church and diocese depended.

"No notice of Bishop Cobbs could do him justice that omitted the fact that he was a man given to hospitality. In him, it was a virtue in excess. There was ever a seat at his table for the stranger and the friend: in his house, guests were never wanting. It was thronged from all parts of the diocese, we might say from all parts of the land. He lived to make others happy, and was never himself so happy as when his bounteous board was crowded with many friends. With his genial spirit and kindly heart, — for in his religion, there was nothing forbidding or morose, — he entered into their feelings, and especially of the young, and made, as well as shared, their pleasure; and a day at the Bishop's was always a day of joy.

"His charity was as unbounded as his hospitality. It was not in his heart to resist any appeal of distress; and with the poor he would have shared his last penny, and his last morsel of bread. There was but one measure to his generosity, — the limit of his means and power. While the barrel of meal wasted not, and the cruse of oil did not fail, whole families of the poor lived upon his bounty; and if his resources were like to be exhausted, he would quietly turn away the word of caution from a friend with 'Jehovah Jireh,' — the Lord will provide.

"The success of the administration of his diocese by Bishop Cobbs was answerable to his great qualities. He found it weak, a Church with no popular prestige, an unsettled and rapidly changing clergy. In the Convention that elected him, but eight clerical names appear on the roll as entitled to a vote and seat. He left it united, vigorous, and growing rapidly in numbers and in strength. An endowed episcopate; a Widow and Orphan's Society, whose vested funds will compare favorably with those of like societies in the older and wealthier dioceses; a flourishing Diocesan School; the parishes more than doubled; the clergy and communicants quadrupled; the alms and oblations many-fold increased; a vigorous system of missions, — these are facts that make his monument, and speak his praise. He was not only a good, but a successful, Bishop, even as the world counts success, by actual results. He was however, a pioneer: his time and labor were spent in laying broad and deep foundations, and not upon the visible walls of the temple. How he labored, what success he achieved, is hidden still in the womb of time; but as long as the Church in Alabama shall have any existence, she will reap the fruit of the toils and prayers of her first-loved Bishop, and her children's children shall rise up to call him blessed."

THE FAREWELL MESSAGE TO THE CLERGY OF THE PROTESTANT EPISCOPAL CHURCH IN THE DIOCESE OF ALABAMA.

"First of all, give to each and every one of them, individually, my love and my blessing; and tell them, that as during my whole episcopate it has been my earnest purpose and constant endeavor to be, and to show myself to be, the personal friend and helper of every clergyman in my diocese, so now I have them all still in my heart.

"As to my religious belief, tell them, that, by God's grace, I shall die in the faith in which I have lived, and which I have endeavored to preach. I have been called a 'Puseyite,' a 'High Churchman,' and the like. Tell them I dislike party names, and loathe party lines in the Church of Christ; but next to Christ, who is the Head, I love the Church, which is His Body, with my whole heart. I have attached, and do still attach, great importance to her offices and sacraments; and I believe in 'Baptismal Regeneration,' and 'Apostolic Succession,' as firmly as I do any of the fundamental doctrines of the Gospel; but I am not conscious that I have ever preached any thing but 'JESUS CHRIST AND HIM CRUCIFIED;' and now, in this solemn hour, reviewing my ministry, I cannot recall a single sentiment, either in my sermons or my pastoral addresses, which I desire erased or changed.

"As to my hope of justification with God, tell them that 'This is a faithful saying, and worthy of all acceptation, that Christ Jesus came into the world *to save sinners.*' I have been called 'a good man,' 'a kind man,' from my youth up. I do not say whether justly or otherwise. I have *tried* to show kindness and sympathy to all, especially to the poor, to the afflicted, and to the bereaved; and I am certain that I do not now bear malice, or cherish unkind feelings, towards anybody on the face of the whole earth. But if I have done any kind deeds or any good works, I am sure I make no merit of them, but cast them all behind my back, and nauseate them, and spit upon them 'as filthy rags;' and, counting myself 'an unprofitable servant,' I look only 'unto Jesus, the Author and Finisher of our faith,' and say,

> 'In my hand no price I bring,
> Simply to Thy cross I cling.'

"As to my present state of mind, tell them I heartily thank God for this sickness. I know not yet what is to be the issue. I have no will nor wish in the matter.

> 'Nor life nor death I crave,'

but simply to do, to bear. to suffer, and to glorify the will of God. This is my sentiment now, and it is the sentiment with which I hope to die.

"And with my farewell blessing upon them, upon their families, upon their parishes, and upon my whole diocese, tell them that their dying Bishop exhorts them to strive to be MEN OF GOD: — men of peace, men of brotherly-kindness, men of charity; self-denying men, men of purity, men of prayer; men striving to 'perfect holiness in the fear of God,' and laboring and preaching with an eye single to His glory and the salvation of souls."

CONCLUSION.

If this book be read by any who hold opposite opinions, it will, I doubt not, be the subject of criticism, and I do not at all deprecate it. If there be any view herein presented that is contrary to the truth, let it perish under rebuke.

By some it will be condemned as calculated to stir up memories of events that should pass into oblivion. Others will say that it does not become an ambassador of the "Prince of Peace" to awaken such memories. To all which, I give for answer, that the proclamation of truth will always arouse the opposition of error, and the enforcement of right will always provoke the antagonism of wrong. All history teaches that no truth has ever gained footing in this evil world save by putting down error, and no right has ever been established save by combating and overthrowing wrong.

This book is "dedicated to the Cause and Maintenance of Truth, Right, and Peace." Truth first, then Peace. There is a peace which results from the triumph of brute force. This is not the peace that should reign among the children of "our Father."

If this, our country, shall ever be fully equipped for her grand mission upon earth, it will only be when mutual respect shall prevail, and when the great principles upon which the late war was waged shall be thoroughly studied, and clearly understood. This cannot be unless every man in his sphere, and from his own stand-point, shall speak out fearlessly, and with more deference to truth than to policy. A peace which is not founded upon mutual respect is an insult on the part of the one section of our country, and a dishonor to the other.

If I did not believe in my heart that the publication of these reminiscences and memoirs would in the end — so far as they have any force — promote the interests of peace, by demonstration of the truth, I would turn these pages into ashes.

It is not sufficient to say — as is commonly said — that "the trouble is now all over, and the country is one and undivided: let us bury in the grave all disturbing memories." This is all very well for the capitalist and the politician. Unhappily, their vocations are not much disturbed by sentiment. There were great moral questions involved in the late conflict. Great men and good men went into the contest with clear heads, warm hearts, and tender consciences, and they have come out of it with the same heads, hearts, and consciences. Have we nothing to learn from such a struggle? Has no truth been established? Is there no moral to such a drama? Was it a fight among brute beasts, that must be " clean forgotten and out of mind"?

Yes, we have one undivided country. For one, I thank God for it. I have never doubted that the restoration of the Union was a great necessity for the welfare of our country. Man plans for the hour: the Almighty Creator plans for the ages. But the recognition of this fact does not at all affect the right or the wrong of the case, moral or political, which is involved in this vast question under review. It is only one of the innumerable examples which history affords of the marvellous wisdom and goodness of Divine Providence, which is ever bringing good out of evil — causing even the wrath of men and the malice of Satan to bring blessings to the children of men. An enemy may thrust me through with a sword, designing my destruction. Instead of striking a vital point in my body, he pierces, we will suppose, a malignant tumor, which has long been an unknown cause of pain and sickness. His thrust gives me renewed life, but he intended my death. I thank a kind Providence which brought good to me out of intended evil. I do not feel any special thankfulness to my enemy. Take an illustration on a larger scale. It was a day of blessing to the brethren of Joseph when, under the pinchings of hunger, they found corn in the land of Egypt, and their brother in the seat of authority. The people of Israel were delivered out of much tribulation. I do not suppose that the brethren of Joseph laid claim to any great merit for having sold him into captivity. Their iniquity, I take it, was none the less for the mighty good which Providence wrought out of their evil. These familiar examples illustrate the great principle, "Fortuna non mutat genus," which, freely translated, may read thus: "The fortunate issue of an enterprise does not change its quality or kind." But the great mass of people disturb themselves very little about the *morale* of their deeds, provided they are successful.

Then, again, as to the question of propriety and decorum on the part of an ambassador of the Prince of Peace in treating of themes which may possibly excite debate and resentment, I have this to answer, — that, personally, the judgment of man has no weight with me. "He that judgeth me is the Lord." Speaking for myself officially, as an ambassador of the Prince of Peace, I have this to say, — that, in all that I have written, I have not been unmindful of the fact that I stand in this relation both to man and the Chief Bishop. He, my Chief, has given me the keynote to my "Reminiscences." I read His proclamation, "I came not to send peace upon earth, but a sword." He who does not know how to interpret this grand and far-reaching truth may be a sincere Christian, and earnest follower of his Lord, but I don't think that he can carry the standard of his Prince into the conflict for great principles. For myself, I should be unwilling to bring out a book (and this is my first and probably last book) which all men would approve, and none would antagonize. There are not only questions of constitutional principle, but deep questions of morals, involved in the matters treated of herein. I was a slaveholder, and an ardent patriot from the Southern point of view. As such, I have nothing to repent of, and nothing to retract. I tried to do my full duty in both of these relations. I have no quarrel with any man, who, from his point of view, considers me, in one of these relations, a violator of pure morality, and, in the other, a rebel against the government. But, whilst I have no quarrel with such a one, I cannot understand how he can pardon my sin without some manifestation of penitence on my part. Treason is a great crime, and a traitor should be hung. How can any one who considers me a traitor fraternize with me, and condone such an offence? Does it not become an ambassador of Christ (and because he represents Christ) to purge himself from the charge of treason by showing justification of his deeds and thoughts?

These are the questions which justify me (speaking as a minister of Christ, and for the ministry of Christ in the South) in setting forth in unambiguous language what I believe in all conscience to be the truth. Should the views expressed in this volume tend in any measure to bring out the truth and the right of the cause which I am vindicating, then is my design accomplished, and I shall hail the peace resulting therefrom as an honorable and enduring peace, — a peace founded in truth and righteousness.

And now, my children, for whose special behoof I have penned these lines, I have but a word more to say. I have treated of difficult and delicate themes. I have used all my endeavors to treat every point with entire candor and fidelity to truth. I am a fallible man, and may possibly have erred in many things treated of. Coming generations must pass judgment upon all our present decisions, and may reverse them all. Should you, in a clearer light than has been vouchsafed to me, reach a conclusion different from mine, then, in the name of Truth, Right, and Peace, cling to your own convictions, ever looking up to the Fountain of all Truth, "The Father of lights," and asking for wisdom to perceive, and strength to maintain, all that you ought to think and to do.

I have mused over this subject many years. " Whilst musing, the fire has burned ; " and at the last I have spoken — God grant — the truth. In naught have I extenuated, nor have I set down aught in malice.

And in full mindfulness of human frailty and folly, I make mine own the language of St. Augustine, —

"*O Domine Deus, quæcunque dixi de Tuo, agnoscant, et Tui; si quæ de Meo, et Tu ignosce, et Tui.*"

MANLINESS.

AT the commencement of this volume, I quoted the words of King David to his son Solomon, "Be thou strong therefore, and shew thyself a man."

I do not know any closing words which would be so apposite as those which tell you what it is to be a man, and what it is to show one's self a man.

My publisher writes me that he is preparing for a second edition of my "Reminiscences," and informs me that I now have an opportunity of adding to them. Since reading the book in print, much has occurred to me which I would like to add in the way of elaboration and illustration. A press of other duties renders this impossible. I cannot, however, forego the opportunity afforded, of giving expression to some thoughts upon a question of vast practical importance to the young men of the coming generation, — "*What constitutes true manliness?*"

The ideal of manliness which each one forms to himself, will depend upon the degree of intellectual and moral elevation to which he may have attained. To the mind of the savage, the successful hunter or the daring warrior presents the highest type of manliness. He is the savage lord, and rules his tribe by dint of a strong arm, and takes leadership as a lion among lions. Hence the names by which the savage chief is called, — "The Lynx-Eyed," the "Swift of Foot," the "Wolf of the Prairie," the "Sitting Bull," etc. Such are the names which give expression to the savage idea of manliness, — names which link him in with the brute, whom he would fain emulate in swiftness, fierceness, and force.

Now, take up your histories of people who have emerged from a state of barbarism, and you meet with names of leaders of men which give expression to higher ideas of greatness and excellence, — "the Wise," "the Good," and "the Just." Always you may mark the elevation of a people by the titles of those to whom they pay highest honor. There is an immense stride from the "Sitting Bull" to Aristides "the Just."

If we come into what we call civilized life, and begin our observation low down in the strata of society, in the atmosphere of saloons and gaming-tables, you will find the successful pugilist the manliest in the ring: muscle, wind, and pluck crown the victor, and encircle him with the girdle of honor. Here, in such atmosphere, grow up the boys, who, with open-mouthed admiration, are learning their lesson of manliness, — to "swear like men," "fight like men," and "take their liquor like men."

Now, come up from these dregs, which lie at the bottom of all our social life, — where riot and debauchery and brute force reign supreme, — and look into a more advanced, but still unregenerate, condition of society. What, in popular estimation, is it, to show one's self a man? Is he esteemed manliest, who, like his Maker, is long-suffering, forbearing, and forgiving? or is it he who maintains the so-called point of honor to the last extremity, who will sacrifice every law, human and divine, to his heated passions, or the demands of a vicious public opinion, and vindicate his manhood by trampling under foot the law of God? See how this spirit flames out in our children scarcely fledged! See how, in their childish brawls, they foreshadow their ideas of a coming manliness!

We are not following the leadings of a sickly sentimentalism in setting forth a standard of higher manliness. Where must we look, to find the most exalted type of humanity? Who was the noblest of the sons of men? There is but One. He stands alone, unapproachable and incomparable. In His presence the most unblushing infidelity stands admiring, if not adoring — Him the Incarnate Word, dwelling among men in the same fleshly tabernacle, environed by the same atmosphere, and encompassed by the same temptations. He who does not feel the supreme necessity of the presence of such an one on earth, not only to reveal God to men, but also to make manifest the ideal man, has learned but little in regard to perfecting his own nature, and comprehends but little of man's greatest needs. I am not now talking to you of theology and creeds. I am speaking of the Man of history, the Man of every age, — the Christ.

Take the greatest man of his era, — the Cæsar Augustus, who ruled the then known world. The chief distinction of that illustrious emperor — all that now survives of his memory — is the fact of history, that, while he reigned, Christ was born. His only fame now is that of the manger and village of Bethlehem, — they indicating the place where, he the time when, Christ was born. They all — prince, village, and manger — serve alike but as landmarks in the track of time, to indicate the beginnings of that kingdom of which there shall be no end. Without prestige of birth, and with "nowhere to lay His head," of obscure life and ignominious death, followed by disciples of no repute, He yet gave birth to a new era in time; and, among civilized peoples, the centuries do now date from His nativity. We cannot discourse of men, and leave out of view the Son of man. As well speak of mountains, and fail to note that which stands loftiest: as well speak of the solar system, and take no note of the sun.

Men may say what they will of creeds and systems of theology and philosophy. They may deny Deity, and deify matter; but they cannot blot out from history, nor dislodge from the hearts of men, the Christ of history, — Him "the Son of man!" No wonder, that, at the inauguration of His mission, the heavens were opened, and a voice from the "Excellent Glory" proclaimed, "This is My beloved Son." Had the heavens been silent, the very stones must have cried out.

There was a deep necessity for the advent of such a Man. The Divine image in men had been defaced, almost obliterated. There were still upon earth the men strong to think, strong to work, strong to fight; but where could you look to find the man who realized in his own life the Divine Image, — the God-mirroring man?

I cannot dwell at length upon that wonderful life of Christ's on earth, and show, as I would love to show, how strong He was to do good, and how strong to resist evil; how sublimely forgetful of self, and how self-sacrificing in His care for others. I touch a single feature of that wondrous character, — His forbearance under provocation and reproach. I single out this particular feature of the manliness of Christ, because it is just here that His example stands out in most striking contrast with the maxims of the world and the passions of men. For, advanced as we may be in morals and self-government, society is as yet at an immeasurable distance from the precepts and example of the Son of man. True it is that we do not, except in our Territories and new settlements, decide questions of title to land, etc., by the strong hand; but an unregulated public opinion still condones, if it does not justify, the appeal to arms in the duel or street-brawl. Still is it true to a lamentable extent, that men are called upon to "show themselves men," and vindicate their manliness, by the exhibition of brute force.

The duel is passing away before the advance of Christian civilization, — chiefly, I fear, because of the political disabilities which a participation in it involves; but there is springing up in its place the street-brawl, in which men find satisfaction for their angry passions. The daily record of these bloody encounters is a blot upon the civilization, not to say the Christianity, of the age. The duel had a touch of chivalry, and originally of piety, in its character; for, in olden times, it was an appeal to God "to show the right." The modern street-brawl is an unmitigated shame. The rules of ancient chivalry allowed that a combat might honorably terminate by the presence, on the field, of a lady, a priest, or the king, — the presence of the latter representing the supremacy of Law. Is the omnipresence of the King of kings no reality to one who has sworn fealty to that Sovereign?

Whence comes that imperious law which holds our men to such a fearful issue; which compels them, as I have often known, to stifle the best feelings of their hearts, to insult the majesty of human law, and to put their sacrilegious hands upon that prerogative which God Himself proclaims, "*is Mine*"? If I know whence it is, it must be because men imagine that their honor — their manliness — is involved. Is this indeed so? Waive all consideration of the reason, the good-citizenship, the piety of it, if possible, does manliness require it? By what rule shall we try this question? Which way shall we go to find it? Shall we go upward, and regard man after that Divine likeness in which he was made? or shall we go downward, and seek in the resemblance which he bears to the lower creation, the source of that unruled passion which impels him, upon every provocation, to resort to brute force in deadly combat?

Here we find it, — low down in the unreasoning passion and brute instinct which locks the beasts of the field in deadly conflict; in the venomous reptile, which strikes its fang into whatever crosses its path or purpose; in the savage state, where one's manliness is measured by his unrelenting hate to an enemy, and his manly prowess by the number of scalps that hang on the walls of his wigwam.

The young Arab — so the story goes — begins to attain the stature of a man. At the accepted time, his father taunts him with being "a woman." The young savage understands too well that he is now called upon to "show himself a man." All the brute within him is stirred. He takes the instrument of death, waits until the shades of night have fallen, and prowls about the tent of some hereditary foe. When his practised ear catches the breathing of assured sleep, he leaps the enclosure, puts his weapon to head or heart: a sure thrust or firm pull makes him "*a man!*" Next morning his tribe greets him "a man;" woman will smile upon him now, and listen to his vows (has she ceased even now to smile upon such men?); and he takes his first degree in a savage manliness.

We have gone low down in the scale of creation: let us go upward, and see how this matter looks from another and higher stand-point.

More than eighteen centuries ago, there was a child born in an obscure village of the East. A wonderful lineage was His — conceived by the Holy Ghost, and born of a virgin mother. As He grew in stature, He grew in wisdom, and in favor with God and man. When He was anointed for His holy mission, God the Father sealed Him. The Divine Spirit descended upon Him in the form of a dove. He came as the Prince of peace to a world in revolt. Lest the symbol of the dove should fail to herald His mission, there came a voice from the "Excellent Glory," and made proclamation, "This is My beloved Son, in whom I am well pleased."

What was the manliness of Him who was thus ushered into the world in the form and with the nature of man? Surely we may learn something from One with whom the Heavenly Father was "well pleased." When He was reviled, He reviled not again: when He suffered, He threatened not. Any man can revile again, when reviled; but how sublime the forbearance which would rather save than destroy an enemy!

When He was at last hunted down by those who would drown in death the voice they could not answer, there was one act of private vengeance, — a follower of His smote a servant of the high priest, and cut off his ear. The crowd around thought, doubtless, that there was one manly man among the disciples; and yet this very man, a few moments later, denied his Master at the taunt of a girl. Christ bore it all; told His follower to put up his sword; stretched forth His hand, and healed the wounded servant; lifted up His voice in prayer for His murderers; in His sublime pity sought an argument for them, — "Father, forgive them: they know not what they do."

We gaze upon this sublime compassion as it merges into the Infinite pity, and the conviction becomes overwhelming that this Son of man was no creation of men's imagining. The mind cannot conceive of that which it has no experience, and for which it has no analogy. The old mythologies create for us men and women like ourselves, with all our little prides and passions. We greet the Christ with an adoring wonder. At infinite distance we strive to follow Him. We would fain sit at His sacred feet, and strive, in our poor way, to be like Him. He is the true man, "Ecce Homo!"

Now go with me from the lowest grade of human nature, — the savage in his war-paint, nursing his hate as a virtue; having no word for forgiveness, because not knowing what it is. Trace this nature as it emerges from the barbarous into the Christian life (and there are men who fear God, and love their fellow-men): trace it through all its gradations of excellence until you reach the Son of man, the "lost Image" of God the Father, and say, "What is it to show one's self a man?"

But men will plead — what will they plead? The necessity of self-defence; the needful limitations of forbearance, where it ceases to be a virtue; the weakness of resolve, and the irresistible force of public opinion. Yes, I am not insensible to the force of such appeals. I know too well what human weakness, under strong temptation, may allow a man to do. But, whatever may be our imperfections, let us not lower the perfection of the Christian standard. Plead, then, whatever you will, of human imperfection, for not being as you ought to be in the way of forbearance, but take care that you plead not *manliness*. For the sake of Him, the manliest, — the Man that would not hurt His fellow-men, but would die, and did die, to do them good, — do not plead *manliness!* If I have wronged another, it is manly in me to confess and repair the wrong. He is not a true man who will not confess his fault. If another has wronged me, it is more than common manliness — it is almost divine — to forgive.

The life of Christ was not a long life, — thirty years of household duty, three of public ministration. Learn, then, this great truth, — that the value of life must be reckoned, not only by its length, but by its depth and breadth; as I have before said, "not only by its *extent*, but by its *intent*."

He accumulated no earthly treasure, but He has left us heirs of all things.

He gained no fame in His day, and yet He founded a kingdom which shall know no end.

His own people rejected Him, and yet generation after generation rise up and call Him blessed.

No tongue, save that of a malefactor, confessed Him when He died; and yet now, myriads of all tongues and climes and ages do bow at the mention of His name.

The moral, then, of the whole, my children, — and with this I close the volume, — is this: Give not much heed to the opinions or judgments of the present hour. A supreme tribunal will review present decisions, and mayhap will reverse them.

The moral of the whole is this: That is the

longest life which in its aims and achievements reaches the farthest ; and that is the manliest life which is the most self-sacrificing and unselfish.

That is the life of Christ, the Way, the Truth, and the Life.

APPENDIX.

Letters of John Stewart referred to in the "Reminiscences."

"RICHMOND, VA., July 27, 1858.

"MY DEAR FRIEND,— Have you accepted any place yet?" (I had several invitations before me at the time.) "I hope not, for I have a plan for your consideration and prayer. It has been long in my head; but I have waited for the removal of obstacles, which Providence has now done. It embraces country-life, farm-employment, plenty of work in God's vineyard in building up a church, and a support while it is going on in its infancy or weakness — given in such a way as not to come in conflict with your entire independence as a gentleman or a minister, or to weaken your hold upon the affection of your congregation.

"Details are for conference, not for a letter. All I can say is, while I am conscious of some selfishness in wishing you for my pastor, yet, as far as I know myself, my main desire is to show my love and gratitude to Him who has done so much for me by bringing His blessed gospel to be preached to the poor black and white around me.

"To insure any chance of success, it is necessary, that, outwardly, I should not be too prominent, but, while you give yourself to your high and sacred duties, it would be my business to see that your support was secured, and secured in such a way that I would not be known in it, and that I could not change it if I would.

"Think over this, and do not hastily throw it aside. If after spreading it, like King Hezekiah, before the Lord, asking and obtaining His counsel, you decide against it, I shall bow to His decision, waiting upon Him to make my path clear.

"I feel now, in every day of idleness or postponement, as if I were one of those 'wicked and slothful servants' whose fate I wish to shun."

Again, under date of 30th of July, he writes thus : —

"I have just had the pleasure of reading your letter hurriedly in this place of business. I write that I was necessarily vague as to details, for in their adjustment my mind would be very elastic to suit all the circumstances which might arise.

"The main thought is this, — that here am I in the midst of a poor heathenized, or rapidly becoming so, population, white and black ; with material all around far more promising to human eye for the formation of an enduring church than in three-fourths of the recently formed country-churches in Virginia; that the natural process being for the gospel to leaven parts adjacent, radiating from the towns as centres until finally it overspreads the length and breadth of the land, why should it not do so, or begin to do so, in the neighborhood of Richmond? I see no reason why it should not be, that, with the proper man, — that is, with love to Christ, and, with Christ, for human souls, with energy, and what is called tact and good sense, good feeling, and a good way of showing all things, so as to draw and touch that strangely complicated machine, the human heart, — we may not ask and look for the blessing of God; and with this, success is certain. Not such as will make much stir or noise in this world, — though, it may be, in heaven, where fame is worth having. I am not blinded by personal attachment when I say that I think you are that man."

And then, again, in his letter of date Dec. 13, 1858, he writes, —

"Yours of the 8th just reached me. While I held it in my hand, before opening it, my heart was lifted to Him 'from Whom cometh our help,' that, if it was an acceptance, His blessing would rest upon His own work, and cause it to prosper; and if it was a rejection, that still His blessing would rest upon His own work, and make my path plain before me what to do, meanwhile waiting patiently for an opening or an indication of what He would have me to do.

"Your letter delivers me from all doubt. My views have undergone no change. Whatever difficulty I may have felt, or modesty in urging, was on your account; for I felt the truth of what you said, that 'your risk was the greatest.' But now that you have decided, and, I believe, have been led by God to decide, I have increased faith and hope that, in spite of the dross which mingled with my motives, He will for His name's sake give us His blessing rich and durable; though it may come, not in the way flesh and blood would like at the beginning. These crosses may be necessary to put out the 'wood, hay, and stubble' which may be mingled with my motives; for, although I am not conscious of *cherishing* any, yet He who searches the heart may see stubble where I only see wheat."

Whoso is wise will ponder these things; and may God give him grace to go and do likewise!

NOTE. — One striking difference, among many others, between Christ and the so-called Vicar of Christ, the Bishop of Rome, deserves to be noted. Christ ever fed the multitudes: it requires multitudes to provide for the wants of His Vicar.

www.ingramcontent.com/pod-product-compliance
Lightning Source LLC
Chambersburg PA
CBHW030818230426
43667CB00008B/1275